THOMAS COOK
Travellers & TUSCANY
FLORENCE

BY
RUSSELL CHAMBERLIN

Produced by AA Publishing

Written by Russell Chamberlin

Original photography by Jerry Edmanson and Ken Paterson

Edited, designed and produced by AA Publishing. Maps © The Automobile Association 1994

Distributed in the United Kingdom by AA Publishing, Fanum House, Basingstoke, Hampshire, RG21 2EA.

The contents of this publication are believed correct at the time of printing. Nevertheless, the publishers cannot accept responsibility for any errors or omissions, or for changes in the details given in this guide or for the consequences of any reliance on the information provided by the same. Assessments of attractions, hotels, restaurants and so forth are based upon the author's own experience and, therefore, descriptions given in this guide necessarily contain an element of subjective opinion which may not reflect the publishers' opinion or dictate a reader's own experiences on another occasion.
We have tried to ensure accuracy in this guide, but things do change and we would be grateful if readers would advise us of any inaccuracies they may encounter.

A CIP catalogue record for this book is available from the British Library.

ISBN 0 7495 0691 1

Published by AA Publishing (a trading name of Automobile Association Developments Limited, whose registered office is Fanum House, Basingstoke, Hampshire RG21 2EA. Registered number 1878835) and the Thomas Cook Group Ltd.

Colour separation: BTB Colour Reproduction, Whitchurch, Hampshire

Printed by Edicoes ASA, Oporto, Portugal

Cover picture: *Duomo Santa Maria del Fiore, Florence*
Title page: *Stepping out in San Gimignano*
Above: *In pursuit of culture*

Contents

About this Book

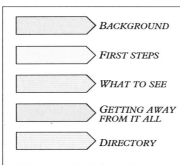

BACKGROUND

FIRST STEPS

WHAT TO SEE

GETTING AWAY
FROM IT ALL

DIRECTORY

This book is divided into five sections,
identified by the above colour coding.

Background gives an introduction to
the country – its history, geography,
politics, culture.
First Steps offers practical advice on
arriving and getting around.
What to See is an alphabetical listing of
places to visit, divided into four regions,
interspersed with walks and tours.
Getting Away From it All highlights
places off the beaten track where it is
possible to relax and enjoy peace and
quiet.
Finally, the **Directory** provides practical
information – from shopping and
entertainment to children and sport,
including a section on business matters.
Special highly illustrated **features** on
specific aspects of the region appear
throughout the book.

Taking time to reflect beside the River Arno

BACKGROUND

'The traveller who has gone to Italy to study the tactile values of Giotto or the corruption of the Papacy may return remembering nothing but the blue sky and the men and women who live under it'.

E M FORSTER
A Room with a View (1908)

Introduction

*D*uring the Congress of Vienna, summoned in 1814 to resettle Europe after the Napoleonic Wars, attention turned to Italy where Napoleon had installed several members of his family as rulers. 'Italy', said Prince Metternich, the Austrian statesman, 'is a geographical expression'. He meant that there was no such thing as an Italian state, even though there was an Italian language and an Italian culture.

Italian civilisation goes back at least 2,500 years, but during that vast stretch of time has only been a single nation for the 400 years of the Roman Empire and for the brief period since Unification which took place in 1870. For most of its history, the peninsula has been divided into a number of small states.

This has been Italy's strength and her weakness. It was a weakness because of the endless bloody struggles that took place between these rival states, and because of their inability to combine against a common enemy. The first foreign invasion of modern Italy took place in 1494 and for the next 400 years the land was a cockpit as the great European states – France, Spain and Austria – claimed this or that part of it for themselves. But the fragmentation of Italy was a strength, too, for out of this diversity came some of the dynamic

tensions which helped to launch the great leap forward we know as the Renaissance.

Modern Italy is still a mosaic of small states under one umbrella and, as fast as you think you have found the final pattern, others pop up from underneath. Milan and Florence may share a

THOMAS COOK'S
Tuscany

Thomas Cook first visited Italy in 1864 and took his travellers to Rome, Naples and to Florence where they stayed at the New York Hotel. An improved rail service from Milan to Florence quickly increased the flow of tourist traffic to the Tuscan capital and Cook, encouraged by this, opened an office in Via Tornabuoni. The wealth of art and architecture to be found in the city attracted many visitors for whom Cook organised special art tours.

In the 20th century Thomas Cook became involved in the transportation of Florentine works of art through their shipping and freight subsidiary companies.

common 'Italian' culture, but they are totally different from each other. Coming down to a smaller scale, Florence and Siena share a 'Tuscan' culture, but again there could scarcely be two more different cities. Coming down to a still smaller scale, Siena is divided into 17 *contrade*, or parishes; while recognising that they are all 'Sienese', each of these has a vigorous, independent life of its own.

These distinctions, together with the local loyalties they generate, are endlessly confusing for the foreign visitor, but they also add immeasurably to the country's cultural richness.

The towers of San Gimignano

History

6th century BC
The Etruscan federation of 12 states (the 'Dodecapolis') is founded: the members include modern Arezzo, Cortona, Chiusi, Fiesole and Volterra.

59BC
Florence is founded by Julius Caesar.

476
The traditional date for the end of the Roman Empire.

774
Tuscany is ruled from Lucca by Frankish counts appointed by Charlemagne.

800
The Frankish king, Charlemagne, is crowned in Rome as the first Holy Roman Emperor.

978
The Badia in Florence is founded by the widow of Uberto, margrave of Tuscany.

Around 1020
Guido d'Arezzo invents musical notation.

1063
Work begins on Pisa cathedral.

1125
Florence conquers and destroys the nearby city of Fiesole.

1152
Work begins on Pisa's Baptistery.

1173
Work begins on Pisa's campanile (the 'Leaning Tower').

1265–1321
Dante Alighieri, author of the *Divine Comedy*.

1289
The Battle of Campaldino between Arezzo and Florence, the last time that citizen-soldiers take part; future battles are fought by mercenaries.

1294
Work begins on Santa Croce church in Florence.

1296
Work begins on Florence cathedral.

1299
Work begins on the Palazzo Vecchio in Florence.

1313–75
Giovanni Boccaccio. The introduction to his *Decameron* provides a vivid picture of the Black Death in Florence.

1334
Giotto begins building the campanile in Florence.

1342
Siena's Palazzo Pubblico is completed.

1348
The Black Death hits Tuscany: in Florence over half the population dies.

1384
Florence conquers Arezzo.

1377
John Hawkwood, the English mercenary, is made Captain General of Florence.

1403
Lorenzo Ghiberti is commissioned to make bronze doors for the Baptistery in Florence.

1406
Florence conquers Pisa.

1434
Cosimo de'Medici returns from exile to begin a 30-year reign as unofficial ruler of Florence, a period of great artistic achievement.

1436
Brunelleschi completes the dome of Florence cathedral.

1469
Lorenzo de' Medici rules Florence.

1452–1519
Leonardo da Vinci, the artist and inventor.

1458
Aeneas Piccolomini, the Sienese cardinal and renowned humanist, is elected Pope Pius II.

1475–1564
Michelangelo Buonarroti, the greatest of the Renaissance artists.

1492
Death of Lorenzo de'Medici who is succeeded by his son, Piero.

1494
Charles VIII, King of France, invades Italy and enters Florence. Because of his failure to resist, Piero de'Medici is expelled from the city.

1494–1512
Florence declares itself a republic under the leadership of Savonarola.

1498
Savonarola is executed for causing civil strife. Soderini takes over as leader of Florence, assisted by Machiavelli.

1500–71
Benvenuto Cellini, the bronze worker, jeweller and autobiographer.

1513
The Florentine cardinal, Giovanni de'Medici, is elected Pope Leo X.

1523
Giulio de'Medici, cousin of Leo X, is elected Pope Clement VII.

1527
Rome is sacked by the forces of the Holy Roman Emperor, Charles V.

1529–30
Having patched up their differences, the Emperor Charles V and the Medici Pope Clement VII combine forces to besiege republican Florence. Florence finally surrenders and Alessandro de'Medici is crowned the first Duke of Florence.

1532
Machiavelli's *The Prince* is published (five years after his death).

1537
Alessandro de'Medici is assassinated. Cosimo I is elected Duke of Florence.

1550
Giorgio Vasari publishes his *Lives of the Artists*.

1557
Cosimo I defeats Siena after a long and bitter siege. Florence now rules most of Tuscany.

1564–1642
Galileo Galilei, the father of modern empirical science.

1570
The title of Grand Duke of Tuscany is bestowed on Cosimo I.

1737
Death of Gian Gastone, last male of the Medici line.

1743
Death of Anna Maria Ludovica, last of the Medici: she bequeaths all Medici property to the city of Florence.

1865–70
Florence is briefly capital of Italy.

1870
The Unification of Italy: Rome becomes the capital.

1940
Italy enters World War II.

1944
Retreating German forces blow up all the bridges of Florence except the Ponte Vecchio.

1946
Italy becomes a republic.

1957
Italy enters the European Community as a founder member.

1966
The Arno floods Florence destroying many works of art.

Geography

*T*uscany provides a textbook example of the old maxim that 'history is a function of geography'; that is, people act in a certain way because of where they live. In the case of Tuscany, mountains have played a formative role. The Appennino (Apennine) range, under different names, curves round the north and east of Tuscany like a protective wall. The region therefore forms a gateway between the north and south of Italy.

Coast and River

On the Tyrrhenian coast, Pisa controls the natural highway formed by the narrow strip of flat land sandwiched between the mountains and the sea. The road that runs down this coastal strip is still called the Via Aurelia, just as it was when the Romans built it nearly 2,000 years ago. Today, the main railway line also runs down this strip.

Over to the east, Florence performs a similar role to Pisa, controlling the passes through the Apenines. In 1944, Field Marshal Kesselring, leader of the retreating German troops, held up the

militarily superior Allied forces by making skilful use of this fact, destroying all but one of the bridges of Florence in order to do so. Historically, Pisa paid the price for Florence's landlocked position: determined to acquire an outlet to the sea, Florence attacked its rival again and again until Pisa was finally conquered in 1406.

The rivers of Tuscany can be both a scourge and a boon for, fed by heavy autumnal rains, they can rise in an alarmingly brief space of time. A vivid indication of the potential danger is provided in Florence and Pisa by the height of the embankments above the normal level of the river. Even this did not protect Florence when, in 1966, the embankments burst and the Arno flooded the city, causing immense damage and loss of life.

Rural Life

Agriculture has, for centuries, been the mainstay of the region. The astonishingly fertile soil produces a great range of crops, including grapes, tomatoes, peppers and aubergines, while the upland pastures are used for grazing sheep that produce the region's famous cheeses. The Monti del Chianti (Chianti hills) provide Italy's best-known wines and Tuscans claim, with justice, that their olive oil is the best in the world. Until World War II, and even as late as

Fertile plots in coastal Tuscany used for growing tomatoes, peppers and aubergines

the 1950s, farming methods had changed little, with oxen providing the main source of power and much of the land farmed on the medieval *mezzadria*, or share-cropping, system. Mechanisation, the reform of land-holding laws and European Community subsidies have since resulted in a rapid alteration of the traditional picture. Even so, some forms of wildlife still flourish; the wild boar (*cinghiale*) is so widespread as to be a pest to farmers – though providing sport for hunters and a favoured addition to the Tuscan menu.

Industry

The beauty of Tuscany's landscape and the splendour of its cities inevitably lead to the whole region being cast as an unspoiled rural idyll. This is by no means the case. Although its industries do not compare in size and variety with those of Lombardy, they are still an important factor. Tuscany is rich in mineral deposits, among them copper,

zinc and alum. The world's largest and best marble quarrries are worked round Carrara. Livorno is one of the Mediterranean region's biggest container ports and the whole Arno valley, between Florence and Pisa, is lined with huge factories manufacturing glass, motorcycles and textiles.

The praiseworthy Tuscan determination to protect the core of its historic cities has not, unfortunately, spread to the countryside. Sprawling developments appear all over the region: little towns, like Greve in Chianti, are smothered in suburban development and Florence now forms one almost continuous conurbation with Prato and Pistoia. Belatedly, a measure of protection is being extended to the countryside. Nature reserves (Parco Naturale) have been established in the mountains of the north, around the Garfagnana, in the south, on the Maremma near Grosseto, and inland around Monte Amiata.

Politics

*I*n September 1992 a wave of general strikes swept over the whole of Italy, their sole purpose being to protest at recent heavy government cuts in social services. In Florence, crowds estimated at more than 100,000 gathered and marched through the streets. They were entirely good humoured, with clowns, stilt walkers and children among their number, but they were also determined.

Italian Communism

Displayed among the red banners of the marchers was the hammer and sickle of the Communist Party. Even after the Soviet Union abandoned Communism, it survived in Tuscany. Italian Communism, admittedly, has always been a rather special form, and one which neither Lenin nor Stalin would have recognised or approved. It is entirely possible for a Tuscan to claim to be both a good Catholic and a good Communist, simply adding to the confusion of Italian politics when viewed from outside.

An Italian word which foreign visitors to Italy would do well to recognise is *sciopero* (prounced 'shioppero') meaning 'strike'. Whereas in many countries strikes are associated with poor industrial relations, in Italy the strike is also a strong political weapon, frequently used to put pressure on the central government in Rome. In order to achieve maximum effect with minimal financial loss to the strikers themselves, a disruptive system of sporadic strikes has evolved; various industries take it in turns to strike between, say, 9am and 12pm, or 3pm and 5pm, or whatever is appropriate. Very little warning is given to the public and one can never be certain whether, for example, a public transport strike will effect both the trains and the buses or just one of these. All the visitor can do is to prepare for the worst and hope for the best.

Antipathy to Rome

A common factor uniting Tuscans of all classes and political views is a dislike and suspicion of Rome, whose bureaucracy is regarded as a quicksand sucking in Italy's wealth and giving nothing in return. In Florence great resentment was caused by a recent central government decree imposing an entrance charge on visitors to the Boboli Gardens. This seemingly minor issue aroused great local indignation because the gardens are one of the few green spaces in the centre of the city, and are much used by mothers with small children. On a wider scale the decree was viewed as a typical example of Rome's interference in local affairs.

Another cause of dissatisfaction is the fact that central government is responsible for the maintenance of most of the major historic monuments in Florence and Tuscany, including churches. There is widespread criticism of the fact that restoration work can trail on for years, or cease entirely when the money runs out, with a harmful effect on the local tourist industry.

Historic Divisions

This dislike of Rome is a reminder that Italy's political unity is increasingly under strain. Unification dates back to 1870, when the kingdom of Italy was created under Vittorio Emanuele II. The Monarchy was abolished in 1946 and a republic created. During the winter of 1992/3 the disclosure of widespread corruption at the highest political levels created a wave of indignation throughout Italy. This culminated in a general referendum on 18 April 1993 when Italians voted overwhelmingly for a fundamental change in Government. A major effect will be the abolition of proportional representation which had contributed to the proliferation of parties, one of the causes of corruption. Future Italian government may well be a form of federation.

Tuscany is currently divided into 20 regions, and it is further subdivided into nine provinces, each named after its capital city: Florence (which is also the regional capital), Arezzo, Grosseto, Livorno, Lucca, Massa, Carrara, Pisa, Pistoia and Siena.

The development of the European Community has given considerable impetus to those political movements that would like to see the north of Italy separated from the poorer south. Their aim would be to create a League of the North which would be independent of Rome and which would, so the argument runs, become one of the most dynamic regions in Europe if freed from bureaucracy and corruption. Some dream of Tuscany being part of this Northern League, while others would go further still and see Tuscany as a completely independent state in its own right.

All the gusto of Tuscan democracy at work on the streets

Italians and Tuscans

*T*he fundamental changes that have taken place in agriculture since the 1940s have deeply affected the people of Tuscany. One of the many Tuscan paradoxes is that these people, who created some of the world's most perfect cities, retained their rural roots. Even today, in the heart of a city, you will come across some patch of vegetables, or a little vineyard, tended by a city clerk in the evenings. The great merchants and bankers of the past made their fortunes in the cities, but always maintained a villa in the countryside – not as a holiday home but as part of an integrated lifestyle. Even the powerful and wealthy ruler of Florence, Cosimo de'Medici, prided himself on his ability to prune his own vines and till his fields.

City and Countryside

At the heart of the Tuscan agricultural system was the *contadino*, the 'countryman', so called because he lived and worked in the *contado*, the cultivated area that lay outside the city walls but which was regarded as part of the city, and which supplied the city with much of its food. The life of the *contadino* has been over romanticised: despite the lush appearance of the Tuscan countryside, the work of a farmer can be brutally hard. Many of these *contadini* did not own the land they farmed. Instead they operated under the *mezzadro*, the so-called 'share-cropping' system which survived into the 1970s; under this scheme, the landowner took half of all the produce grown on this land as rent. The *mezzadro* had many faults, but it also ensured that the *contadino* had a

direct stake in the land. Today, he is more likely to be an agricultural employee, financially better off, better housed (probably in one of the ever-expanding suburbs) but with no interest in the soil that he ploughs.

Incomers and Tourism

Harsh farming conditions meant that many people abandoned farming as a way of life once the mezzadro system was abolished. This retreat from the land is most evident in the hundreds of villas which have been turned into hotels, and the thousands of farmhouses which have become second homes for wealthy urbanites from Florence, Siena, Rome and Milan. One entire locality has gained the slightly pejorative name of 'Chiantishire' because of the large number of British who have moved in (although, in reality, there are just as many Germans, Dutch and even Americans as British living here). Tourism, at first regarded as a lucrative alternative to backbreaking farm work or hand-to-mouth retailing, is now proving a problem because of the sheer number of visitors pouring into the region. The innate courtesy of the people who live in rural Tuscany, their amused interest in

foreigners, means that human contact is still made, but with increasing difficulty.

An Enigmatic People

Italians are perhaps the most self-contradictory people in the world. Passionately individualistic, they are also the people who have evolved the concept of 'the city' in its most perfect form, as a place where co-operation is the vital prerequisite. Their prolonged feuds and vendettas are legendary – a well-known proverb runs: 'Revenge is a dish best eaten cold'. At the same time they can be almost embarrassingly hospitable to a stranger. They are the people who once elected 'La Cicciolina', a soft-porn actress, to parliament, yet they are also the people for whom the family is, quite literally, sacred.

They also invented the whole idea of *machismo*, but, as the Italian journalist Luigi Barzini wrote in *The Italians*, his lighthearted but highly perspicacious survey of his fellow countrypeople: 'Men run the country – but women run men. Italy is in reality a crypto-matriarchy.' Do not expect to understand Italians in a fortnight, or a year, or even a lifetime. It is doubtful if they understand themselves.

The Tuscans

What is true of Italians is even truer of Tuscans. They are a race of farmers and merchants, neither of them trades that are usually known for their concern with aesthetic values, yet they not only sponsored some of the world's most perfect art, they also triggered off the artistic revolution of the Renaissance which, in turn, profoundly influenced the art and architecture of the rest of the Western world.

In a country where local patriotism

Swapping gossip at the market

counts far higher than national, Tuscans claim to have the deepest roots. They point out proudly that DNA tests show that they are indeed descended from the ancient Etruscans, and they seize on any characteristic which distinguishes them from the despised Romans – even claiming that Tuscan roads are interestingly winding while Roman roads are boringly straight. Their fellow Italians regard them with some wariness – the Florentines in particular, with their sharp tongues and sharper business sense. Some visitors find them friendly, others somewhat haughty, but this is because they regard their city as the best on earth. The best way to get on with any Florentine is simply to agree with this judgement and flatter them outrageously.

The Etruscans

The Etruscans remain one of the most enigmatic of ancient peoples. They dominated central Italy from around 900BC until they were conquered by the Romans in the 3rd century BC. At the height of their power, Etruscan influence spread as far south as what is now Naples and as far north as Ravenna. We can see their tombs all over Tuscany, notably in Chiusi, and the foundations of an entire city at Roselle, just outside Grosseto. There are at least 10,000 inscriptions in their language, written in a script which has affinities with Greek. We even know the names of some of their leaders: Lars Porsena, who led the attack on Horatius defending the last bridge to Rome, was a real person, the King of Chiusi at the beginning of the 6th century BC. Legend has it that his tomb lies in a vast labyrinth somewhere beneath Chiusi. We know all this, but we still do not fully understand their language, nor do we know from whence they came; were they indigenous to Italy, or did they come as immigrants from the East?

One reason why we know so little is because their cities and many of their artefacts were of wood and hence have not survived. Another is that the Romans deliberately suppressed and effaced Etruscan culture after the 3rd century BC. As a result, most of our knowledge about their lifestyle comes

The golden light of dawn falls on Populonia's Etruscan tombs

from their tombs and this has resulted in something of a one-sided picture, so that some writers have deduced that they were preoccupied with death. This is certainly not borne out by the exquisite wall paintings found in some of those tombs. The Etruscans were formidable warriors, as the Romans sometimes found to their cost, but they also seem to have enjoyed life to the full. The tomb paintings feature dancing lovers, young men playing the flute, delicate country scenes. Most moving of all are the three-dimensional figures carved on their sarcophagi. Frequently these show a husband and wife, not grieving but seated as at a banquet, lovingly touching each other, smiling as they drink wine.

The Etruscans, though courageous and skilful, were ultimately crushed by the brutal military efficiency of Rome. The English writer, D H Lawrence, believed that they nevertheless triumphed in the end: 'Rome fell, and the Roman phenomenon with it. Italy today is far more Etruscan in its pulse than Roman, and will always be so'.

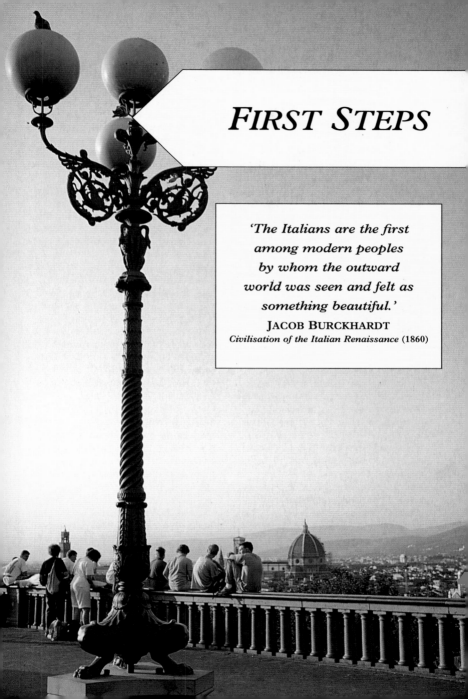

FIRST STEPS

'The Italians are the first
among modern peoples
by whom the outward
world was seen and felt as
something beautiful.'
JACOB BURCKHARDT
Civilisation of the Italian Renaissance (1860)

Tuscany: a land of artisans

TOURIST OFFICES

On arriving in a Tuscan city for the first time, your first port of call should be the local tourist office (the addresses and telephone numbers of the major offices in Tuscany are given in the **Practical Guide**, see page 189). Tourist office staff are usually efficient and courteous, and most have a working knowledge of French, German and English. They will provide free maps and a range of well-produced leaflets, either free or sold for a nominal sum. A major limitation of many tourist offices is that they know little and care less about the neighbouring provinces.

THE SIESTA

One matter in which the Italians have entirely declined to accommodate visitors is that of opening (or, to be more precise, of closing) hours. Everything

shuts for three hours in the middle of the day and some sights are only open in the mornings. Shops, tourist offices and museums all put up their shutters sometime between 1pm and 4pm. Although there is a growing tendency for the more important museums and galleries to open again in the afternoon, these are few and far between.

There is only one infallible rule in response to this situation: when in Rome, do as the Romans do – and the Florentines in Florence and the Pisans in Pisa and, in short, Italians everywhere in Italy. Your options are to put off lunch for as long as possible, then find a comfortable *trattoria* in which to while away the afternoon hours (restaurants are one of the few types of establishment which do not close); or you can take a picnic to some green and shady spot; or you can just go back to your hotel for an unabashed siesta. The world will come back to life again at about 5pm and you will, by then, be refreshed enough to enjoy it.

CASH DESKS

Fiddling the books to cheat the tax man is a universal Italian custom and to combat it almost every transaction is supposed to be accompanied by an official receipt. Thus, in the larger city bars, unless you are seated at a table, you must first go to the cash desk (*cassa*) and give your order. On paying you will be given a receipt and this you present to the barman who will then serve you (in busy bars you will get better service if you put down a 100 lira coin with your receipt!). The same procedure applies to certain shops, such as delicatessens, where it can create complications if you want a variety of purchases or do not know the Italian name of the goods you want to purchase. The best way round this is to shop or drink in smaller, corner-shop establishments where the service is more personal.

BUS TICKETS

Another variation on the 'pay before you use' system is the obligation to obtain your ticket before you board a bus. There are no conductors and the driver's job is simply to drive; this is a good idea, in terms of road safety, but presents problems for the unwary. Tickets are obtainable in most tobacconists and bars (they are also available from machines at major bus stops in cities such as Florence). It is a good idea to buy several at a time, since nothing is more infuriating than to find yourself in some remote part of a city where the only local bar has run out of tickets. On the bus you must 'cancel' the ticket by inserting it in a machine which will stamp it with the date and time. If you are caught without a ticket, or with an unstamped ticket, you will be fined 30 times the fare, and no excuses accepted. Tickets last for one hour from the time they are stamped, allowing you to change buses.

LANGUAGE

The Italians are an extremely tactile people who use vigorous body language to back up their verbal language and frequently touch the person to whom they are speaking. Do not take offence at this. On the other hand be wary of that minority of males who still act the Latin lover, pursuing females with or without invitation. Italian women have long since learned to deal with this nuisance with a torrent of contemptuous abuse, a tactic not open to most foreign visitors. The only real defence is to ignore the advances completely.

Outside the big cities and tourist centres, fewer people speak a foreign language. They are, however, delighted if you make even the most halting attempts to speak Italian. Tuscany is acknowledged, even by other Italians, as having the purest form of the language, with the purest Italian of all spoken in Siena. Italian grammar is complex but many people find the pronunciation easier than other European languages. Many Tuscans pronounce 'c' as 'h' so that *seconda* becomes *sehonda*. With a few exceptions, however, each word is pronounced exactly as it is spelt, with the stress usually on the penultimate vowel (see **Practical Guide**, page 184). Speak slowly and clearly and you should be understood.

In Florence's Piazza della Signoria

TUSCANY

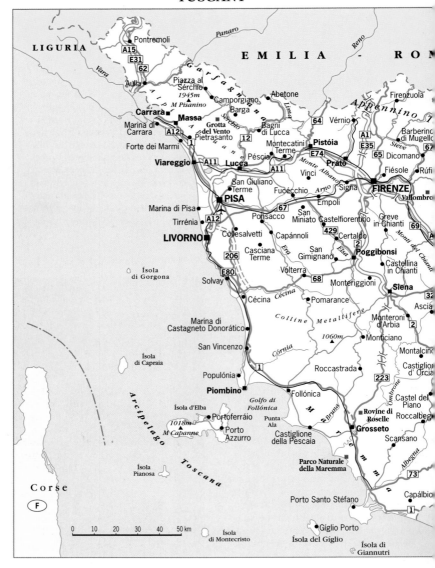

CITY LIFE

Florence is the only really big city in Tuscany, with a population of nearly half a million. Livorno comes a long way after with a population of around 180,000: then comes Prato at around 165,000, followed by Pisa with about 105,000, and then Arezzo, Lucca and Pistoia at around 90,000 each. All the rest are delightfully small and intimate: it is possible to walk across the entire width of Siena, for instance, in under half an hour.

Italian town planning has ensured that the historic centres of all cities – the areas of interest to most tourists – are largely untouched, although the surrounding suburban sprawl can be rather horrible. Even in a city as big as Florence, therefore, you can simply step out of the train or bus and start wandering round in the city centre as though it were a small town.

There is not much nightlife in any of the cities – except for Florence, Pisa and the seaside towns – but most people find it enough to sit at a pavement café in one of the incomparable squares and watch the world go by. That, after all, is what the Italians themselves like doing best.

COUNTRY LIFE

Tuscany is blessed equally with some of the most beautiful cities in Italy and one of the most beautiful landscapes in the world. Even with a big city like Florence it is possible to get into open countryside within 10 minutes or so by bus. Maps are, unfortunately, not very accurate and footpaths are rarely signposted so cross-country walking is not to be undertaken casually. Following the lanes, however, is a delight, while the mountains to the north provide spectacular vistas and, in most parts, quite easy walking.

CAMPANILISMO

Sienese *contrade* symbols and
the cathedral bell tower

For more than 1,500 years, from the fall of the Roman Empire until 1870, Italy had no central government. Region fought against region, city against city, even village against village. The only safety lay behind the walls of your own city or *comune*. Crammed behind those walls, the citizens were forced to live together, developing urban skills, lavishing their best on the public buildings of the *comune*. A medieval lawyer said: 'Man is born first to God and then to the *comune*: he who hurts the *comune* hurts God'. Traitors to the *comune* suffered an appalling death – they were buried alive, upside down – 'like a stake'.

The great symbol of the *comune* was the campanile, the bell tower. Here hung the great bell which was used to summon the citizens to public assemblies. When an emergency struck, whether an attack from outside the walls or a rebellion within, the bells would be rung *a stormo*; in other words, with a tremendous discordant clattering which brought the citizen militia hurrying to

their posts. When the French King Charles VIII threatened Florence in 1494 declaring he would sound his trumpets to signal the attack on the city, the Florentines retorted, 'If you sound your trumpets we will ring our bells'.

From that concept there developed the quite untranslatable idea of *campanilismo*. Roughly this means excessive attachment to the city (or even the parish) of one's birth. The concept of local patriotism is still strong and takes its most extreme form in the city of Siena, which is divided into 17 parishes, or *contrade*, each named after a bird or an animal. Each of the *contrade* has its own church, its own social centre, its own museum and its own banner or *gonfalon*. Each has an open-air shrine where the symbol of the *contrade* – whether it be the panther, or the goose, or the elephant – is erected. Competition between the *contrade* can be seen at its most intense at the city's celebrated Palio (see page 150), the bareback horse race between jockeys from each of the parishes, that takes place in summer.

'In the distant plain lay
Florence, pink and gray and
brown'.
MARK TWAIN, *AUTOBIOGRAPHY,*
(1892)

Firenze (Florence)

Seen from the surrounding hills, Florence seems the perfect example of a romantic Italian city. The warm red-gold roofs nestling in the bowl of the hills, the silver ribbon of the River Arno winding through, the enormous cathedral presiding majestically over its flock, the stern tower of the Palazzo Vecchio soaring up as guardian – all these come together harmoniously to make an enchanting picture.

Brunelleschi's soaring cathedral dome – the tallest structure in Florence

Fortress City

Despite this, on entering the city itself the first impression is often one of claustrophobia. This is partly due to Florence's history. It was one of the most democratic – but also one of the most turbulent – of Italian city-states, with factions endlessly fighting for dominance. Those who could afford it turned their homes into fortresses which still give a grim appearance to the narrow streets. Occasionally, when the great street door of one of these palaces opens, you may catch a glimpse of a walled garden or a courtyard within, hinting that the dour exterior does not tell the whole story – but, for the most part, Florentine buildings do seem very austere and forbidding.

Modern Florence is also a booming industrial city with a population of nearly half a million. The historic centre inevitably comes under pressure, particularly from traffic. Florentines argue that this is the price you pay for a city that remains very much alive. Although the city is one of the world's major tourist attractions, drawing in two million people annually, it is still a working city. Even in the historic centre you will find small workshops where furniture is made or bicycles are repaired, side by side with four-star hotels or luxury jewellers.

Mercantile City

Florence has always been like this. In the Middle Ages and the Renaissance Florence owed its great wealth, which allowed it to become the major cultural capital of Europe, not to some all-powerful prince but to its workers and merchants and bankers who built upon the foundations of a thriving wool and textile trade. So confident were foreign traders in the wealth and integrity of Florentine merchants that their gold coin was accepted as a common European currency. That coin was called the *florino* after the city's Roman name *Florentia*, which appeared on the obverse. The name florin entered most European languages.

The Florentine virtues during the great formative years of the city were the virtues of merchants – prudence and restraint. Even so, they lavished superb works of art on their sacred buildings and created several big set pieces which every visitor comes to see: the Duomo (Cathedral), the Piazza della Signoria and the Ponte Vecchio. These are usually as crowded as a railway station in the rush hour and the visitor who sees only these areas may well carry away a rather jaundiced view of the city. If you have time, however, you only need to

turn aside down one of the narrow streets, whose width and course has remained unchanged for centuries, to find the real life of the city.

Artistic contortions in the Galleria dell'Accademia

ACCADEMIA, GALLERIA DELL' (THE ACADEMY GALLERY)

The Academy was founded by a group of artists in 1563, the first school of art in Europe. It is now the Florentine School of Art. The Academy Gallery was founded by Grand Duke Pietro Leopold in 1784 to house casts and models used by the students. At the entrance to the gallery, on Via Ricasoli, you will almost certainly find a long queue, for the Accademia is synonymous with Michelangelo's *David*, one of the top attractions of Florence.

Michelangelo was only 29 when he completed this important piece of work. The statue is carved from a single block of Carrara marble that had been rejected by other sculptors and had lain around for over 40 years before Michelangelo got to work on it. It was finished in 1504 and, like so much Florentine art, it had

FLORENCE TOWN PLAN

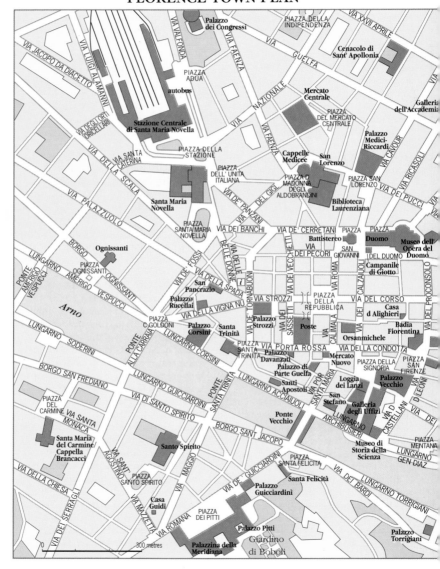

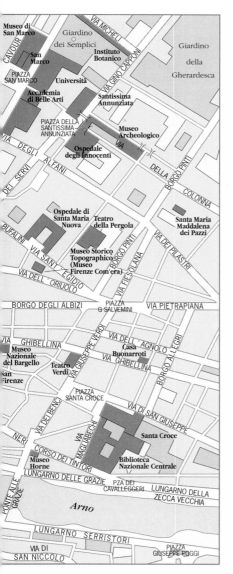

a political purpose: David signifies the Republic triumphing over the Goliath of tyranny. The statue was originally placed in the Piazza della Signoria; in 1873 it was removed to the Accademia and a copy installed in its place. The *David* has virtually become a logo for Florence, but it has not been universally admired. The 19th-century English essayist, William Hazlitt, described it as 'like an awkward overgrown actor at one of our minor theatres, without his clothes'.

In the same room are Michelangelo's four *Slaves*. Unlike *David*, which is finished to such a chill perfection as to leave little room for the imagination, the *Slaves* are unfinished and are deeply poignant. Each of the giant figures, contorted in despair, seems to be trying to break free from the block of marble which still imprisons it. You can still see the marks of the chisel which was slowly shaping the figure on each block. Originally intended for the immense tomb of Pope Julius II in Rome, Michelangelo worked on them for nearly 17 years, between 1519 and 1536. There has been endless debate about whether they really are unfinished works; perhaps Michelangelo intended to leave them like that, to symbolise the soul escaping from the body.

Michelangelo's work inevitably dominates, but there is much else to see in the Accademia, including some magnificent 16th-century tapestries and paintings ranging from the 13th to the 18th centuries, including work by Perugino, Taddeo Gaddi and Filippino Lippi.

Via Ricasoli 60 (tel: 055 214 375). Open: Tuesday to Saturday, 9am–2pm; Sunday 9am–1pm. Admission charge. Nearby: San Marco.

THE RENAISSANCE

The Renaissance in Italy is generally assumed to have begun in the early 14th century in Florence – but what exactly was it? Scholars have been debating the question for over a 100 years and are likely to continue to do so. Some argue that there was no such thing as 'the Renaissance' and that the period was simply one more evolutionary stage in the continuum of European history. Others argue that 'the' Renaissance was actually 'a' renaissance – in other words, one of many, just like the earlier ones that took place in Carolingian Europe in the 8th and 9th centuries and in France in the 12th century.

Where the Italian Renaissance differs is that people *at the time* knew that something remarkable was happening, that a profound redirection of thought was taking place. The great scholar Petrarch, writing in the 1350s, said, 'I stand as a man between two worlds'. The word 'rebirth' itself was coined while the process was happening and the word first appeared in print in

1550 when the Florentine art historian, Giorgio Vasari, claimed that his book, *Lives of the Most Excellent Painters, Sculptors and Architects,* would help readers 'to recognise more easily the progress of art's rebirth (*rinascita*)'.

What Vasari meant was that Florentine artists were involved in a revival of the ideas of ancient Greece and Rome, which were then being re-discovered in long-lost manuscripts. This was later extended to include first architecture, and then what we now call science and technology. In 1855 a

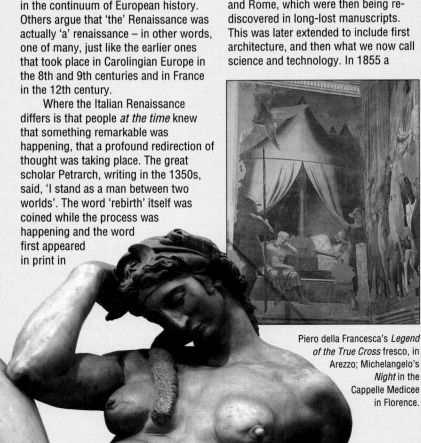

Piero della Francesca's *Legend of the True Cross* fresco, in Arezzo; Michelangelo's *Night* in the Cappelle Medicee in Florence.

Top left and right: Ghirlandaio's *Nativity* in Santa Trinità church and his statue of *Winter* on Ponte Santa Trinità, Florence

French historian picked up the idea of a rebirth of classical ideas but translated it into French, and thus as 'Renaissance' it has gone down in history.

In many a Tuscan art gallery, especially those whose paintings are arranged chronologically, it is possible to follow the new trend in art as the formal religious paintings of the Middle Ages gradually give way to paintings of mythological subjects, scenes from

Below: Ghiberti's golden Baptistry doors, in Florence

daily life or paintings that are still religious in context but more realistic in the portrayal of human emotions. The best gallery in which to see this development is the Uffizi in Florence (see page 62). In architecture the Renaissance is evident in the change from the Gothic buildings of the Middle Ages to classical structures derived from the study of Roman architecture. The Rucellai Palace in Florence (see page 52) is a good example of the latter. In literature writers such as Petrarch and Boccaccio turned away from an endless preoccupation with theology, 'the study of God', to humanism, 'the study of man'. These three trends put together changed the face of Tuscany and, within a few years, had sparked off similar movements in many parts of Europe.

BADIA FIORENTINA (THE ABBEY OF FLORENCE)

It is said that Dante used to haunt this ancient church (founded in 978, rebuilt in 1285) in order to feast his eyes on Beatrice, the girl he idolised in the *Divine Comedy*. He would still recognise the Romanesque campanile although much of the church was rebuilt again in 1627. At first sight the interior seems empty and uninteresting but there are two superb works of art. On the left-hand wall in front of the altar is the tomb of Ugo, Margrave of Tuscany (died AD1001), son of Willa, who founded the abbey in memory of her husband, Uberto. The tomb itself is a Renaissance masterpiece, sculpted by Mino da Fiesole in 1469–81. The other great work is a painting, *The Madonna Appearing to St Bernard* by Filippino Lippi. To the right of the choir a stair-case leads to the *Chiostro degli Aranci* (the Cloister of the Oranges) where the monks once grew orange trees. The walls are decorated with 15th-century frescos on the life of St Bernard.
Via del Proconsolo. Open: daily, 9am–noon: 4pm–6pm. Admission free. Nearby: Bargello.

BARGELLO, MUSEO NAZIONALE DEL

Few buildings sum up Florence's embattled past so well as this grim fortress in the heart of the city. Begun in 1255, the Bargello served as the city's first town hall. Later it was used as a law court and then, in 1574, it became the headquarters of the Chief of Police. The portraits of convicted criminals were displayed here and sometimes their bodies as well, following their public execution in the courtyard.

The Bargello became a museum in 1859 and now houses one of Italy's most important collections of sculpture. Although not as overwhelming as the Uffizi, it is still advisable to allow at least two hours to view the collection.

Despite the Bargello's grim history, the courtyard, with its *loggia* and grand staircase, is beautiful. The ground floor (entrance on the right) contains work by Michelangelo (1475–1564), Cellini (1500–71) and other late Renaissance artists. Michelangelo's sculptures include the drunken *Bacchus*, his first free-standing statue, and the noble

The Bargello's stately courtyard

Brutus – the only bust he ever made. Look out for Cellini's exquisite little preliminary model for *Perseus slaying Medusa*. Beside it are the original panels from the finished statue, now displayed in the Loggia dei Lanzi (see page 59).

Ascending the grand staircase from the courtyard will take you up to the loggia which has been turned into a charming aviary for the bronze birds of Giambologna (1529–1608). The door on the right is the entrance to the immense *Salone del Consiglio Generale* (General Council Chamber). This was originally the law court and now contains the most important works of the early Renaissance. Outstanding even in this company is the work of Donatello (1386–1466), including his *David* (1408), the first statue in the round made since the time of the Roman Empire. In this room, too, are the trial panels showing *The Sacrifice of Isaac* made by Ghiberti and Brunelleschi in the Baptistery doors competition (see page 34). Other rooms on this floor contain a priceless ivory collection, a collection of Islamic art and Byzantine jewellery. The floor above houses a stunning display of the ceramic work of the Della Robbia family.

Via del Proconsolo 4 (tel: 055 210 801). Open: Tuesday to Saturday, 9am–2pm; Sunday, 9am–1pm. Admission charge. Nearby: Badia Fiorentino.

BIBLIOTECA LAURENZIANA (LAURENTIAN LIBRARY)

The entrance to the library is through the cloister of San Lorenzo church (see page 40). The library was designed by Michelangelo to hold the vast number of priceless manuscripts collected by Cosimo de'Medici and his grandson, Lorenzo. The manuscripts were removed

Giotto's elegant campanile

to Rome but were brought back by the Medici Pope Clement VII who commissioned Michelangelo to build the library in 1524. The seats and reading desks, and even the lists of manuscripts on the side of the desks, are exactly as Michelangelo designed them.

Piazza San Lorenzo (tel: 055 210 760). Open: Monday to Saturday, 9am–1pm. Admission free. Nearby: San Lorenzo.

CAMPANILE DI GIOTTO (GIOTTO'S BELL TOWER)

Although universally known as 'Giotto's Tower', he was only responsible for the first storey, begun in 1334. The rest of the work was undertaken by Andrea Pisano (died 1348) and completed by Francesco Talenti. The extraordinary multi-coloured marble and Gothic tracery ensures that the tower stands out

among the surrounding sober buildings, and only the cathedral and Baptistery can compete with it. Like so many of Florence's outdoor sculptures, the originals of the panels which decorated the tower are now in a museum, the Museo dell'Opera del Duomo. The ascent to the top of the tower is fairly easy and provides a spectacular view – but it should only be undertaken by those with a good head for heights.
Piazza del Duomo. Open: summer, daily, 9am–7.30pm; winter, daily, 9am–5pm. Admission charge. Nearby: Duomo, Battistero.

CAPPELLA BRANCACCI (BRANCACCI CHAPEL)

In 1423 Felice Brancacci, a wealthy Florentine diplomat, decided to follow

Strolling across the River Arno; the spiritual side of Florence

the fashionable trend and pay for the decoration of a chapel in his local church. He chose an established artist, Masolino. Masolino's 22-year-old assistant was called Tommaso di Ser Giovanni di Mone; the Florentines, with their love of nicknames, called him Masaccio – meaning 'Hulking or Loutish Tom' – presumably because of his appearance. The assistant rapidly became the master and he created a series of frescos which do for painting what Ghiberti's Baptistery doors do for sculpture: they mark the moment when the Renaissance broke free from the Middle Ages.

Most of the panels tell the life of St Peter, turning him into a real, living person instead of the remote god-like figure of earlier art. Perhaps the most famous of all Masaccio's scenes is the *Expulsion of Adam and Eve* which makes a complete break with every previous presentation of the subject. Adam has buried his face in his hands in utter despair while Eve is screaming in terror. It is interesting to compare this treatment with Masolino's treatment of the same subject on the opposite wall. The frescos, after long neglect, were brilliantly restored between 1984 and 1990.
Piazza del Carmine (tel: 055 212 331). Open: Monday, and Wednesday to Saturday, 10am–5pm; Sunday, 1pm–5pm. Admission charge. Nearby: Santo Spirito.

CASA BUONARROTI (MICHELANGELO'S HOUSE)

Michelangelo (whose surname was Buonarroti) bought this house in 1508 but never lived in it, regarding it simply as a useful investment. It was his nephew Leonardo who, after inheriting the house in 1564, began to develop it as a kind of shrine to the memory of his famous uncle. In 1612 Michelangelo Buonarroti the Younger extended the house and commissioned a number of artists to create imaginary pictures of the life of the great man. The house first opened as a Michelangelo Museum in the mid-19th century.

Despite its tenuous connection with Michelangelo himself the museum provides an invaluable insight into his life and work. The most important exhibits are on the first floor, including Michelangelo's earliest known work, the sculptural panel called *The Madonna of the Staircase*. There is also a wooden model of Michelangelo's design for the façade of San Lorenzo, though this was never built.

Via Ghibellina 70 (tel: 055 241 752). Open: Wednesday to Monday, 9.30am–1.30pm. Closed Tuesday. Admission charge. Nearby: Santa Croce.

CASA DI DANTE ALIGHIERI (DANTE'S HOUSE)

Although this is an entirely modern reconstruction on an historic site, it is well worth a visit as an honest attempt to recreate a 13th-century house. On display are editions of the *Divine Comedy* as well as Botticelli's illustrations to the poem. Whether or not Dante was born in a house on this site, this is certainly his home ground. Just across the narrow street is the church of Santa Margherita de'Cerchi where, it is said, Dante was married, while near by is the Badia Fiorentina, the parish church of his great love, Beatrice.

Via Santa Margherita (tel: 055 283 343). Open: Thursday to Saturday and Monday to Tuesday, 9.30am–12.30pm and 3.30pm–6.30pm; Sunday, 9.30am–12.30pm only. Closed Wednesday. Admission free.

Heaven, Hell, Dante and Florence

DANTE ALIGHIERI (1265–1321)
When Dante decided to write his epic poem the *Divine Comedy* in the Tuscan dialect, instead of the universal scholarly language of Latin, he gave the 'people's language' a tremendous boost. His three-part poem describes his journey through Hell, Purgatory and Paradise and is a curious mixture of political propaganda, mysticism – and personal spite: he took great pleasure in placing his enemies in Hell and devising suitable eternal punishments for their 'sins'. Dante was exiled from Florence in 1302 as a result of one of the city's many political upheavals and he spent the rest of his life wandering round the courts and monasteries of northern Italy. He died in Ravenna where he is buried. There are proposals from time to time to return his remains to Florence but it is unlikely that they will ever succeed. Florence, however, sends an annual gift of oil to Ravenna for the lamps around his tomb.

Battistero San Giovanni (Baptistery)

*B*uilt some time between the 5th and the 8th century on Roman foundations, this is the oldest surviving building in Florence. As late as the 15th century, indeed, the Florentines claimed that it had once been a temple to Mars, founded by Julius Caesar. This is the sacred building most revered by the citizens of Florence. According to custom, on 21 March all children born in the city over the previous 12 months were brought here to be baptised.

The elegant green and white marble cladding of the exterior was added between the 11th and 13th centuries, and it served as a model for other Florentine churches. The interior is richly decorated, incorporating Roman columns and capitals. The self-confident Florentines did not hesitate to call on the artists of other cities to embellish their beloved Baptistery: the Byzantine-style mosaic in the ceiling is probably the work of Venetian artists while the

The octagonal Baptistery, the oldest surviving building in Florence

decoration of the font is Pisan. The only other object in the interior is the exquisite tomb, designed by Donatello, of the 'antipope' John XXIII (Baldassarre Cossa) who was deposed in 1414.

But beautiful though the interior is, the three sets of bronze double doors are what set the Baptistery apart from any other building in the world. The South Doors are the oldest. They were made by Andrea Pisano around 1330 and the 20 panels at the top tell the story of Florence's patron saint, St John the Baptist, while the bottom eight show the Virtues.

The North and East Doors are among the most important objects in the history of modern art for they mark a key moment in the development of Renaissance techniques, such as naturalistic perspective. In 1402 the wealthy Guild of Cloth Merchants of Florence decided to celebrate the city's delivery from plague by commissioning a new set of doors, the North Doors. A competition was organised, another 'first' in art history and seven leading artists were invited to submit a panel on the same subject, *The Sacrifice of Isaac.* Two artists, Lorenzo Ghiberti and Filippo Brunelleschi, were eventually judged to be the joint winners (their original panels are to be seen in the Bargello). The Guild suggested that they work together to create the new doors but Brunelleschi refused and went off, in high dudgeon, to study classical architecture in Rome. The 25-year-old Ghiberti thus began his single-handed work on the doors; he started in 1403 – and did not finish them until 21 years later. The Guild were so pleased with his work that they immediately commissioned another set of doors for the eastern portal. Ghiberti spent the next 27 years on these, from 1425 to 1452.

Both sets of doors are staggering in their detail and execution. The North Doors consist of 28 panels surrounded by Gothic quatrefoils, representing the Life of Christ and the Evangelists in a manner which is far removed from the formalism of the Middle Ages. The East Doors (facing the cathedral) consist of only 10 panels but these are the doors which Michelangelo described as the 'Gates of Paradise'. The panels you see now are casts of the originals (which have been removed for cleaning and subsequent display in the Museo dell'Opera del

The 'Gates of Paradise'; the east doors of the Baptistery

Duomo). Even so, the reproductions clearly show Ghiberti's genius and his work is better seen here than in a museum. The subjects of the panels are taken from the Old Testament and scenes such as the *Creation of Adam and Eve* are illustrated in a lively, realistic style. Ghiberti also departed from tradition by including portraits of his contemporaries, in the guise of prophets and sibyls, around the frames. He even put his own self-portrait there: he is the fourth down on the right-hand side, a balding man with a rather self-satisfied smile (the similar figure next to him is his father).

Piazza del Duomo. Open: daily, 1pm–6pm. Admission free.

Florence Churches

OGNISSANTI (ALL SAINTS)

Ognissanti was the parish church of Amerigo Vespucci, the man who had the entire continent of America named after him. Founded in 1256, the church was completely rebuilt in 1627 in the baroque style that was then in fashion, although the campanile is medieval. The interior of the church is richly decorated in the rather lush manner of the period but contains work by Botticelli (who is buried here) and Ghirlandaio. The Vespucci family tomb is below the second altar on the right. Ghirlandaio's painting over the altar, the *Madonna of Mercy*, supposedly contains a portrait of Amerigo himself – he is the boy peering

THE VESPUCCI FAMILY

The Vespucci were a wealthy family of merchants, who dealt mostly in luxury clothing and wine. Despite their wealth they were closely identified with this predominantly working-class quarter. Amerigo (1451–1512) worked for the Medici as an agent in Spain and in 1499 he made a voyage across the Atlantic as a result of which he proved that Columbus had discovered a 'new world' and not the eastern shores of India as he had supposed. The first maps of the new world were based on Vespucci's account of his voyage, published in 1504, and because of this the lands previously known as 'Mundus Novus' were called 'America' after the Latin version of Vespucci's Christian name.

from behind the man in the dark cloak. Above the altar opposite is Botticelli's *St Augustine* (1480).

Another work by Ghirlandaio is to be found in the Convent next to the church (entry through the cloister); the Refectory holds his great fresco of the *Last Supper* (1480).

Borgo Ognissanti (tel: 055 239 8700). Church open: daily, 9am–noon and 3pm–6pm. Refectory open: Monday, Tuesday and Saturday, 9am–noon. Admission free.

ORSANMICHELE

The Italian habit of truncating words and running them together has given this church its unusual name, which contains a clue to Florence's past. Between the 9th and 13th centuries there was a garden here (*orto* in Italian) with a church alongside called San Michele ad hortum (St Michael by the garden). This church was latter replaced by a loggia which was used as a trading hall. In 1380, the loggia was enclosed and two upper stories were added, giving the building its present odd appearance, for it looks more like a tower than a church. At this point, the ground floor was once again used as a church, while the upper floors were used as an emergency grain store.

Each of the city's guilds was given responsibility for decorating one of the niches in the outside wall of the church and from this developed the present astonishing display of statuary, since the guilds strove to outdo each other by commissioning outstanding artists of the day. Some of the statues have been moved to museums and replaced by copies. Among the most important are:

(east side) Ghiberti's *John the Baptist* (1416), the first full-size Renaissance statue in bronze; *Doubting Thomas* by Verrocchio (1483); (north side) *St George* (1416) by Donatello (this is a copy; the original is in the Bargello); Nanni di Banco's *Four Crowned Saints* (1415); (west side) Ghiberti's *St Matthew* (1422); *St Eligius* (1414) by Nanni di Banco (the bas relief below shows some of the saint's miracles); (south side) Donatello's *St Mark* (1411).

The interior is as oddly shaped as the exterior and is very dark. Its outstanding feature is the tabernacle in glass and marble by Orcagna (1359) which glows like an immense jewel in artificial light. Access to the upper storeys is by a footbridge from the Palazzo dell'Arte della Lana opposite.
Via dei Calzaiuoli (tel: 055 284 715).
Open: daily, 9am–noon and 3pm–6pm.
Admission free.

Bernardo Daddi's radiant *Madonna* framed by angels in Orsanmichele church

1564. Next is Dante's cenotaph. It is empty because Dante never returned to his native city after he was exiled in 1302; instead he died and was buried in Ravenna, and Florentines still send an annual gift of oil for the lamps around his tomb.

Just beyond Dante's 19th-century cenotaph is an 18th-century memorial to Niccolo Machiavelli (died 1527), author of *The Prince* and Secretary to the Republic before it was overthrown by the Medici. Between the two, on the nearby nave pillar, is a pulpit by Benedetto da Maino (1476), regarded as one of the

In Santa Croce (left) frescos by Taddeo Gaddi and (below) the 14th-century sanctuary

SANTA CROCE

Begun in 1294 and intended to be the largest church in Christendom, the basilica of Santa Croce was finally completed in the 19th century when the façade was paid for by the British benefactor, Sir Francis Sloane. The vast interior features nine chapels at the eastern end, each one named after one of the immensely wealthy banking families of the city who paid for its mural decorations. These frescos, including some by Giotto, are among the most important medieval works of art in Florence.

The church is also Florence's Pantheon – the burial place of the city's outstanding men. Starting at the main entrance from Piazza Santa Croce, the first tomb on the left-hand side (north aisle) is that of Galileo who was originally refused burial within the main church, but whose body was moved here in 1737. On the opposite side (the south aisle) the first tomb is that of Michelangelo who died in Rome in

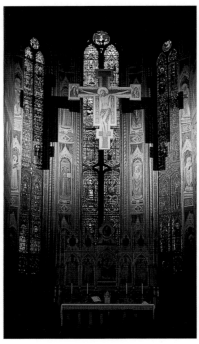

most perfect of the Renaissance. Then comes a beautiful *Annunciation* in gilded limestone by Donatello (around 1430), while high up on the wall just beyond is the perfect Renaissance tomb of Leonardo Bruni (died 1444), the scholar who wrote the first history of Florence.

The two chapels on the right-hand side of the high altar are the Bardi and Peruzzi chapels, both decorated by Giotto and his pupils in the 1330s. The frescos have deteriorated because Giotto painted on dry plaster, instead of wet, and the paint eventually flaked off in places. Their condition became so poor that they were whitewashed over in the 18th century and forgotten for over 150 years before being restored in 1959. The

Bardi chapel (next to the altar) contains scenes from the life of St Francis of Assisi; though not as striking as Giotto's famous frescos on the same subject in Assisi, scenes such as the *Death of St Francis* show the artist's mastery in depicting human emotions. The fifth chapel to the left of the high altar (the Bardi di Vernio) was frescoed by Giotto's follower, Maso di Banco, with *Scenes from the Life of St Sylvester* (late 1360s).

Off to the right-hand (south) side of the main altar is a passageway that leads to the Sacristy, dominated by a tremendous 14th-century *Crucifixion* by Taddeo Gaddi.

Housed in the old monastic buildings adjoining the basilica is the Museo

GIOTTO

Giotto (1266–1337) was the first artist in medieval Italy to break away from the formality of Byzantine-inspired art; by adopting a more realistic approach to the depiction of figures and landscapes, he laid the foundation for the art of the Renaissance. Giotto was born in a village near Florence and was the son of a peasant farmer. According to Vasari, Giotto learned to draw as a shepherd boy by scratching pictures of sheep into the rocks – hence the idea that Giotto's naturalism came from his study of nature. Even allowing for the fact that Giotto was helped by numerous pupils and assistants, his output was astonishing; his most famous work is the St Francis fresco cycle in Assisi, but his work is also to be found in Rome, Naples, Bologna, Padua and Florence.

Santa Croce church rises from a sea of red roofs

dell'Opera di Santa Croce with works by Cimabue, Donatello and Orcagna. *Basilica, Piazza di Santa Croce (tel: 055 244 619). Church open: Monday to Saturday, 8am–12.30pm and 3–6pm; Sunday, 3pm–5.30pm. Admission free. Museum open: summer, 10am–12.30pm and 2.30pm–6.30pm; winter, 10am–12.30pm and 3pm–5pm. Closed Wednesday all year. Admission charge.*

SAN LORENZO

Looked at from outside it is difficult to imagine that this battered, unfinished church situated in a rumbustious and inelegant marketplace was the 'family church' of the wealthy and powerful Medici. Inside it is a different story. Designed by Brunelleschi and built between 1419 and 1469, it was the the very first church to be built in Renaissance style in Florence. Its details are important not just in the history of art but also because they relate to the Medici and reflect the history of Florence over three centuries.

The peaceful cloister alongside San Lorenzo church

The great nave is a cool and classically harmonious work in grey stone. High up on their individual pillars are two great bronze pulpits by Donatello (*c*1455), the last of his works and commissioned by his great friend Cosimo de'Medici to give him employment in his old age. Just beyond, a multi-coloured marble roundel in the floor marks the spot where Cosimo himself lies buried. He died in 1464 and his epitaph simply says *Pater Patriae* (Father of his Country), the title

bestowed upon him by the city council after his death, and the same title once given to Cicero by the Roman senate. In the crypt below the very last of the Medici, Anna Maria Ludovica, also lies buried. On her death in 1743 her will revealed that she had left everything the Medici owned to the citizens of Florence, which explains why the city is such a treasure house of art today.

On the left of the high altar is the entrance to the Sagrestia Vecchia (the Old Sacristy). Built by Brunelleschi in 1421–9, and decorated with reliefs by Donatello, this contains the tomb of the founder of the Medici family wealth, the banker Giovanni di Bicci de'Medici (died 1429) and that of Donatello himself.

Piazza San Lorenzo (tel: 055 216 634). Open: daily, 8am–noon and 3.30pm– 5.30pm. Admission free. Nearby: Biblioteca Laurenziana, Cappelle Medicee.

CAPPELLE MEDICEE (MEDICI CHAPELS)

Although attached to San Lorenzo church, the Medici Chapels have a separate entrance in the Piazza Madonna degli Aldobrandini

The grandest of the chapels, the Cappella dei Principi is entered first. This was commissioned by the Grand Duke, Cosimo I, and designed by Buontalenti who began work in 1605. The vast marble mausoleum, designed to display the wealth and power of the later Medici, was not completed until 1737. The pavement and walls are inlaid with coloured marbles and semi-precious stones – lapis lazuli, mother-of-pearl, coral and porphyry.

The Sagrestia Nuova (New Sacristy) was commissioned by the Medici Pope Leo X and the contrast between this

the city in 1531. A small chamber below has more sketches discovered after the great flood of 1966.

Piazza Madonna degli Aldobrandini (tel: 055 213 206). Open: Tuesday to Saturday, 9am–2pm; Sunday, 9am–1pm. Closed Monday. Admission charge.
Nearby: San Lorenzo, Biblioteca Laurenziana.

The Cappelle Medicee; (above) the sumptuous tomb of Grand Duke Ferdinand; (right) Michelangelo's *Dawn* and *Dusk*; (below) the chapel entrance

serene, harmonious chapel and its vulgar neighbour is total. This is not surprising for both the sculptures and the architecture of the Sacristy are the work of Michelangelo (1520–34). Ironically, the two tombs which carry four of his most famous sculptures commemorate little-known members of the Medici family. On the right is the sarcophagus of Giuliano, Duke of Nemours, who died in 1516. The figures which crown the tomb are known as *Day* and *Night*. Opposite is the tomb of Lorenzo, Duke of Urbino (died 1519) crowned by the figures of *Dawn* and *Dusk*.

In the little room behind the altar in the sacristy, perspex sheeting covers some rough sketches in charcoal made on the wall by Michelangelo and discovered in 1975. He probably hid in this room when the Medici reconquered

THE MEDICI

The Medici family ruled the city of Florence almost continuously for over 300 years, from 1434 until the death of the last of the Medici, Anna Maria Ludovica, in 1743. At first they wielded power but without holding any official office or title. Later their position of absolute power was acknowledged when Alessandro was crowned the first Duke of Florence in 1530 and Cosimo I was made the first Grand Duke of Tuscany in 1569.

Two of the most important members of the family were Cosimo 'Il Vecchio' ('the Old'), who ruled from 1434 until his death in 1464, and his brilliant grandson Lorenzo 'Il Magnifico' ('the Magnificent') who ruled from 1469 until he died in 1492. Cosimo used his enormous wealth as a banker to build such monuments as San Lorenzo church and the monastery of San Marco. He himself was a scholar and he paid for other scholars to collect and translate ancient Greek and Roman manuscripts, including the works of Plato and Cicero; by this means he was instrumental in encouraging renewed interest in the classics, one of the defining characteristics of the Humanist age.

Lorenzo assumed the leadership of the family and the city at the age of 20 when his father (Piero the Gouty) succumbed to an early death in 1469. Lorenzo was reluctant to take up the reins of power but, as he said frankly: 'It fares ill in Florence with any who

Piero de'Medici, father of Lorenzo

possess wealth without any share of the government'. Lorenzo soon proved himself a worthy and able leader in the same mould as his grandfather, Cosimo. Though physically an unattractive man, with a sallow skin, a great beaky nose and a harsh squeaky voice, he was immensely popular among all classes. He was himself a gifted statesman, poet, musician and philosopher, and he was capable of recognising genius in others – among the many artists whom he encouraged was the young Michelangelo. His death at the early age of 43 was a tragedy for Florence.

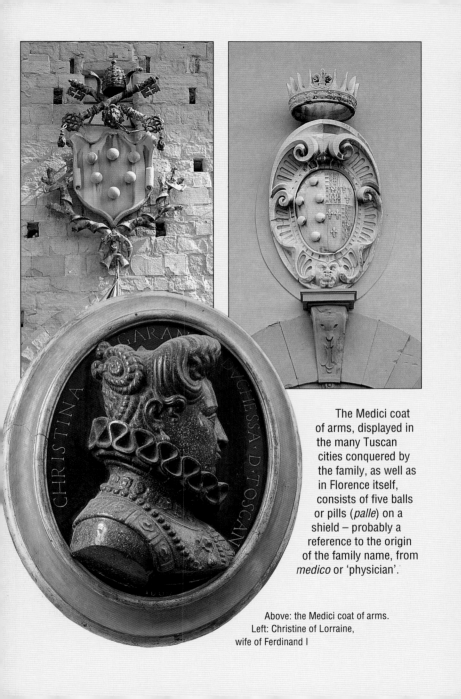

The Medici coat
of arms, displayed in
the many Tuscan
cities conquered by
the family, as well as
in Florence itself,
consists of five balls
or pills (*palle*) on a
shield – probably a
reference to the origin
of the family name, from
medico or 'physician'.

Above: the Medici coat of arms.
Left: Christine of Lorraine,
wife of Ferdinand I

this was one of the first paintings to make full use of the new science of perspective.

Behind the high altar is a charming fresco series painted by Ghirlandaio with the help of his assistants, one of whom was the young Michelangelo. The frescos depict scenes from the lives of the Virgin and of St John the Baptist but almost all the scenes are set in the Florence of the time, thus providing a marvellous insight into the social life of the 15th-century city. The women present at the births of St John and the Virgin Mary, for instance, are ladies of the Tornabuoni family who commissioned the frescos.

The cloisters to the left of the church also have a spectacular range of frescos. Several of the scenes on the life of Noah were painted by Paolo Uccello, who was literally obsessed by the mathematics of

SANTA MARIA NOVELLA (ST MARY THE NEW)

This enormous church was built in the late 13th century by the Dominicans. They were proud of the pun on their name – *Domini cane* (Hounds of the Lord) – for it was they who hounded heretics through the Inquisition. Thus it is that the frescos in the Cappellone degli Spagnoli (the Spanish Chapel) in the cloister show the Dominicans as black and white dogs, those being the colours of their habits. It was in this church, from the pulpit designed by Donatello, that Galileo was denounced for teaching that the earth went round the sun and not the other way round.

Santa Maria Novella is particularly famous for its frescos. On the left-hand wall of the nave is *The Trinity* by Masaccio. Painted in 1428, a year or so before his death at the tender age of 27,

Santa Maria Novella: (top) the façade; (above) Ghirlandaio's frescos

The classical purity of Brunelleschi's Santo Spirito church

linear perspective, spending hour upon hour in making complex calculations. He used a green pigment which gives a ghostly hue to his awesome picture of *The Flood* with its tragic victims (1431).
Santa Maria Novella, Piazza Santa Maria Novella (tel: 055 210 113). Open: summer, daily, 7am–11.30am and 3.30pm–6.30pm; winter, daily, 4pm–6pm only. Admission free.
Cloisters, Piazza Santa Maria Novella (tel: 055 282 187). Open: Monday to Thursday, 9am–2pm; Saturday and Sunday, 8am–1pm. Closed Friday. Admission charge (free Sunday).

SANTO SPIRITO (HOLY SPIRIT)
Santo Spirito is well worth a visit because it is the last major work of the great Renaissance architect Filippo Brunelleschi. He prepared a model for the church in 1428 and work was in progress by the time of his death in 1446. The façade was never completed, hence its disappointing front, but the perfect classical harmony of the interior is as Brunelleschi intended. There are paintings by Verrocchio and Filippino Lippi in the transepts.

Piazza Santo Spirito (tel: 055 210 030). Open: summer, daily, 8am–noon and 3.30pm–6.30pm. Winter, daily, 4pm–6pm. Admission free.

SANTA TRINITÀ (HOLY TRINITY)
Founded in 1092 but rebuilt between 1258 and 1280, Santa Trinità is famous for a miraculous crucifix and vivid pictures of social life in 15th-century Florence. The crucifix is in the chapel on the right of the altar and, according to tradition, nodded approval to a young man who forgave his brother's murderer. The adjoining Sassetti Chapel has frescos by Ghirlandaio. As with his frescos in Santa Maria Novella these scenes incorporate contemporary people and settings. On the altar wall are scenes from the life of St Francis set in the Piazza della Signoria and in Piazza Santa Trinità, while the figures include Lorenzo de'Medici ('the Magnificent'), his sons and their tutors.
Piazza Santa Trinità (tel: 055 216 912). Open: Monday to Saturday, 7am–noon and 4pm–7pm; Sunday, 4pm–7pm. Admission free.

Duomo Santa Maria del Fiore (Cathedral)

*T*he first sight of the exterior of the Cathedral of Santa Maria del Fiore (Holy Mary of the Flowers) may come as a shock because its multi-coloured marbles hover on the brink of an almost fairground garishness. Three different coloured marbles have been used: white from Carrara, red from the Maremma and green from Prato.

The cathedral was begun in 1296 as a deliberate challenge to the great cathedrals then rising in Pisa and Siena: the Florentines announcing that their cathedral would be the greatest building in the world 'surpassing anything built by the Greeks and Romans'. The first architect, Arnolfo di Cambio, drew up a plan and construction work went well for over a 100 years. The building was nearly complete by 1418 – all except for

the enormous dome. Nobody had any idea how the huge space was to be covered without incurring vast expense in timber and scaffolding. After endless anxious debate the authorities decided to let Filippo Brunelleschi build the dome – though not without some hesitation because Brunelleschi declined to say how he would accomplish the task, except that he promised no scaffolding would be used. Brunelleschi succeeded, using a cantilevered system, to raise what was then the biggest dome in the world. It took 16 years to complete and even today is surpassed in size only by St Peter's in Rome. The lantern was planned by Brunelleschi but only added in 1461, sometime after his death, and it has stood the test of time despite fears that its weight would bring the whole dome crashing down.

As with so many Florentine churches, the façade was left unfinished. The present confection was made in 1888 and is already in need of renovation. The marble was obtained by explosives, instead of by the traditional method of sawing and, critics say, this weakened its molecular structure causing the façade to deteriorate.

The interior of the building is huge – contemporary reports claim that at least 10,000 people crowded in to hear the sermons of Savonarola. The proportions

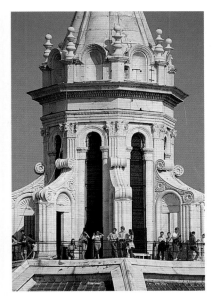

death the Florentines atoned for his exile by instituting a series of public readings of his work, held in the cathedral at Easter. The background to this painting shows Paradise and Inferno as Dante envisaged them – and the major buildings of 15th-century Florence.

It is possible to ascend to the summit of the cathedral dome, though this should only be attempted by those with a very good head for heights; the gallery is narrow and the balustrade is only waist high. The crypt is also open to the public (on payment of a separate admission charge); it contains Roman remains and the foundations of Santa Reperata church which was originally built in the 4th century but which was demolished to

Climbing to the top of the cathedral dome provides an unforgettable new perspective of the city below

are majestic but the colouring is a rather depressing brown, only coming to life on feast days when the great columns are hung with crimson banners.

Ironically, two of the most prominent works of art are portraits of mercenary soldiers; both are on the left-hand (northern) wall of the nave. They depict Niccolo da Tolentino and the Englishman Sir John Hawkwood who became Captain-General of Florence in 1377 (see page 98). The Florentines had promised him a memorial in the form of an equestrian statue but they fobbed off his heirs with this fresco (1436) by Paolo Uccello instead. Uccello used his great skill in perspective to create this chiaroscuro picture, which gives the appearance of a three-dimensional statue.

Just beyond, on the pillar on the right, is a painting of Dante. After Dante's

make way for the cathedral in 1296. Here, too, you can see Brunelleschi's simple tomb; he is the only person ever to have been buried in the cathedral. *Piazza del Duomo (tel: 055 294 514). Open: daily, 10am–5pm. Admission free. Crypt and dome (tel: 055 230 2885). Open: Monday to Saturday, 10am–5pm. Admission charge. Nearby: Campanile di Giotto, Battistero.*

Florence Museums

MUSEO ARCHEOLOGICO (ARCHAEOLOGICAL MUSEUM)

Housed in a 17th-century palace, this vast collection – which includes exhibits from ancient Egypt, Greece and Rome as well as Tuscany – was once admirably labelled and displayed. The museum suffered badly in the 1966 flood and the effects are still being felt. Some rooms are still closed and elsewhere the exhibits are being rearranged. Sensibly, the authorities have concentrated on restoring and displaying the more famous and popular exhibits, many of which are again on view in enhanced conditions.

The museum was begun by the Medici and the core of the collection comes from the bequest of the last of the Medici, Anna Maria Ludovica. As a result, the museum has some of the finest Etruscan treasures to be seen outside of Rome. Most of these are displayed on the ground floor and pride of place is given to the *Chimera*, part lion, part goat, part snake, cast in bronze in the 5th century BC. The bronze was discovered in Arezzo in 1555 and promptly claimed by Cosimo I. Near by is the *Arringatore*

(Orator), another fine Etruscan bronze portraying a member of the Metelli family and made in the 3rd century BC when Etruscan aristocrats had already begun to adopt a Roman lifestyle. A rich collection of funerary objects includes a cinerary urn carved in the form of an Etruscan house and found near Chiusi. There are also some outstanding Greek vases and an Egyptian room containing a very well-preserved chariot made of wood and bone.

Via della Colonna 36 (tel: 055 247 8641). Open: Tuesday to Saturday, 9am–2pm; Sunday, 9am–1pm. Closed Monday. Admission charge. Nearby: Accademia.

MUSEO DELL'OPERA DEL DUOMO (CATHEDRAL WORKS MUSEUM)

Almost every Italian cathedral has transferred some of its more vulnerable treasures to a museum, but Florence has carried this to extremes. Heavy pollution perhaps justifies stripping the exterior of the Baptistery and the Campanile but much has been removed from the interior of the cathedral as well.

Hence to this museum you must come if you want to see the original panels made by Ghiberti for the Baptistery East Doors; the panels are being put on display as they are restored. Here too are the sculptured panels that originally decorated the lower stages of the Campanile,

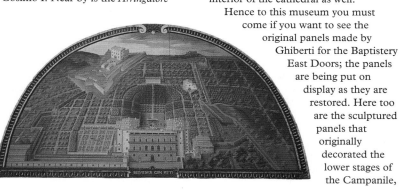

Museo di Firenze com'era: (left) the Pitti Palace; (above) the Pianta della Catena

admittedly much easier to study here at eye-level than high up in their original position.

Particularly interesting are the statues which Arnolfo di Cambio made for the planned façade of the cathedral which was never built. There is also a small exhibit illustrating the construction of the dome, together with Brunelleschi's death mask. Donatello's sculptures from the Campanile are here together with his choir loft from the cathedral. Michelangelo's agonised *Pietà* (the Virgin holding the body of Christ) has been given accommodation here during the long task of restoring the dome. The bearded figure of Nicodemus, who assists the Virgin, is said to be Michelangelo's self-portrait.
Piazza del Duomo 9 (tel: 055 230 2885). Open: summer, Monday to Saturday, 9am–7.30pm; winter, 9am–6pm. Closed Sunday. Admission charge.

MUSEO DI FIRENZE COM'ERA (MUSEUM OF FLORENCE AS IT WAS)

This museum is mainly devoted to plans, maps, topographical drawings and paintings of Florence. It traces the physical development of the city from the 15th century onwards. One outstanding exhibit is the immense reproduction of the so-called *Pianta della Catena* (Chain Map) of 1470, the original of which is in Germany. This is not a map as such but a meticulous bird's-eye view of Florence, probably painted from the viewpoint of Bellosguardo, the hill just to the south of the city. A photograph taken from the same viewpoint today would show an astonishing degree of similarity.
Via del Oriuolo 24 (tel: 055 239 8483). Open: Monday to Wednesday, Friday and Saturday, 9am–2pm; Sunday, 9am–1pm. Closed Thursday. Admission charge.

PALAZZO DAVANZATI (MUSEO DELLA CASA FIORENTINA ANTICA)

The moment you step into the vestibule of this museum you will receive a vivid impression of the violence of life in 14th-century Florence. This is not simply a palace but a fortress – or even a prison. The four square holes in the ceiling overhead were made to enable the palace occupants to pour boiling pitch or lead on unwelcome guests. The massive inner doors lead into a stone courtyard with a well. Access to the living quarters above is by a narrow, easily guarded staircase.

The palace was built in the mid-14th century and occupied, unchanged, as a family home until 1838. In 1905 it was acquired by an antique dealer, named Elia Volpi, who furnished it as a Florentine home would have appeared in the 14th century. Although decidedly dark, the palace is surprisingly comfortable and indeed homelike. There is even a serving hatch, moving up through the floors to the kitchen on the upper floor, and two bathrooms.

The Sala Grande (Grand Room) on the first floor is laid out like a drawing room. Next door is the dining room, the Sala dei Pappagalli (Room of the Parrots), so-called because of the parrots which appear on the walls, cleverly painted to resemble tapestries. The walls of the main bedroom on this floor also have intricate wall decorations.

The bedroom on the upper floor has an example of a *cassone* – the chest which a Florentine bride received for setting up her household – which is filled with rare linen of the period. The wall painting in this room illustrates a French

Ghirlandaio's *Last Supper* in San Marco's refectory

SAVONAROLA

It is a profound irony that San Marco, decorated by the gentlest of friars, should later become the headquarters of one of history's most fanatical monks, Girolamo Savonarola. His portrait hangs in his cell at the end of the dormitory corridor. It shows a forceful, ugly but intelligent face, with a great beak of a nose and burning eyes. Born in 1452, Savonarola came to the monastery in 1489 and gained an immense reputation for his fiery sermons. He proclaimed that his task was to cleanse Florence of its sins and he vigorously attacked the powerful Borgia pope, Alexander V, for his crimes.

In 1494 the people of Florence rebelled against the Medici, disgusted with the cowardice of Piero de'Medici who did nothing to resist the French invasion of the city. Savonarola then became virtual ruler of the newly declared Florentine Republic and instituted a fanatically puritanical regime. At first he carried many Florentines with him – they even built enormous 'Bonfires of the Vanities' on which priceless works of art and luxuries, such as mirrors and fine clothes, were burned. Eventually, however, the Florentines tired of his excesses and abandoned him to his enemies. In 1498 he and two companions were hanged and burnt in the Piazza della Signoria.

Savonarola died on this spot

medieval romance. The kitchen is on the top floor, as were all kitchens of the period, to reduce the risk of fire. It is fully equipped with antique vessels and kitchenware.

Via Porta Rossa 13 (tel: 055 216 518). Open: Tuesday to Saturday, 9am–2pm; Sunday, 9am–1pm. Closed Monday. Admission charge.

SAN MARCO, MUSEO DI

San Marco was originally built in 1437 as a convent, funded by Cosimo de'Medici and designed by his favourite architect, Michelozzo. It was also equipped with the first ever public library in Europe. Today San Marco is virtually a display case for the frescos of Fra Angelico who was a friar here in 1436–47 and, with the help of various assistants, painted devotional scenes on the 44 cells of the dormitory. Fra Angelico's luminous, gentle works bridge the gap between the Middle Ages and the Renaissance for although the subjects are formal and religious, the figures are vibrant with life.

Unforgettable is the *Annunciation* which greets the visitor at the top of the steps leading into the dormitory quarters. In this painting Fra Angelico shows the stunned expression of a young woman who has just been told that she is to be the mother of God.

Piazza San Marco 1 (tel: 055 210 741). Open: Tuesday to Saturday, 9am–2pm; Sunday, 9am–1pm. Closed Monday. Admission charge.

Florence Palaces

PALAZZO MEDICI-RICCARDI

This was the home of the Medici family for over 100 years. Lorenzo the Magnificent was born here and it was here that he reluctantly took over the leadership of the city at the age of 20. Kings and emperors were entertained here and it still discharges an important role for the building now houses various local government offices. Most of it is open to the public, however.

Built between 1444 and 1460 by Michelozzo for Cosimo de'Medici, it is a typical example of Florentine understatement. It is also characteristic of the prudence of the early Medici that the palace, large though it is, is set along the street line like an ordinary house. The exterior has three distinct storeys, the ground floor being in the 'rusticated' style very popular in Florence. Stone benches, on which petitioners once waited, are still in place.

Much of the interior was changed and enlarged by the Riccardi family who bought the palace in 1659. An elegant arcaded courtyard leads to a pleasant formal walled garden. A lift will take you up to the gallery, a remarkably vulgar confection painted in 1683 by the Neapolitan artist, Luca Giordano. The Riccardi probably intended to compliment the Medici by commissioning these scenes glorifying the later members of the clan. Far more attractive is the great fresco depicting the *Procession of the Three Magi* which occupies three walls of the chapel. Painted by Benozzo Gozzoli in 1459, it has a joyous, springtime feel about it. It is also an invaluable historical record because Gozzoli included several members of the Medici family and their contemporaries in the scene. The immensely long procession, complete with camels, is shown winding its way up a hill in Tuscany. The young king on a white horse in the foreground is an idealised portrait of Lorenzo the Magnificent. His brother Giuliano, who was later murdered, is depicted just behind the black man with a bow. Alongside the bowman, on horseback, is their grandfather, Cosimo, and next to him their father Piero. Gozzoli put himself in the picture as well, just behind the Medici; he ensured his immortality by writing his name in gold letters on his red hat.

Via Cavour (tel: 055 217 601). Open: Monday, Tuesday and Thursday to Saturday, 9am–1pm and 3pm–5pm; Sunday 9am–noon. Closed Wednesday. Admission free. Nearby: San Lorenzo.

PALAZZO DI PARTE GUELFA

After they had destroyed their opponents, the Ghibellines, in 1266 the Guelfs were the dominant political party in Florence. The party acquired this property as their headquarters in 1277, enlarged it over a century and then, in 1418, commissioned Brunelleschi to design the present palace, in which he incorporated much of the old. Though not open to the public, the exterior is worth seeing.

Via delle Terme. Nearby: Ponte Vecchio.

PALAZZO RUCELLAI

Although not so well known as the Medici palace, this is perhaps more important architecturally as it was one of the first of the Florentine palaces to be

The inner courtyard of the Palazzo Medici-Riccardi

designed on classical principles. It was built for the rich merchant Giovanni Rucellai by the scholarly architect Leon Battista Alberti who drew on his researches in Roman architecture. Today it houses the Alinari Photographic Museum.
Via della Vigna Nuova (tel: 055 213 370). Museum open: Thursday to Tuesday, 10am–7.30pm. Closed Wednesday. Admission charge. Nearby: Santa Trinità.

PALAZZO STROZZI
Although work started on this palace in 1489, only 45 years after the Medici palace, it nevertheless belongs to a different era. Unlike the reticent Medici palace, the Strozzi palace is brutally domineering. Its purpose was to display the power of Filippo Strozzi, the great banker whose wealth rivalled even that of the Medici. For over 15 years Strozzi stealthily bought up property in the city centre, eventually acquiring 15 houses which were demolished to make way for this monster. Building work went on for over 46 years, long after Strozzi's death in 1491. A permanent exhibition on the ground floor illustrates the development of the palace, which is today used for trade fairs and conferences.
Via Strozzi (tel: 055 215 990). Open: Monday, Wednesday and Friday, 4pm–7pm. Admission free.

The fortress-like Pitti Palace seen from the Boboli Gardens

PALAZZO PITTI

This is the least Florentine of all the palaces in the city because of its aggressive display. Now housing several museums, the Palazzo Pitti was built from 1457 for Luca Pitti who was deliberately trying to outrival the Medici. Indeed, the plans of the palace were originally offered to Cosimo de'Medici when he was planning the construction of the Palazzo Medici, but he turned them down as being far too ostentatious. Ironically, after the Pitti's wealth declined they had to sell the building to Eleonara di Toledo, wife of the Medici duke, Cosimo I, in 1549. Cosimo moved in 1550 and from then on it served as the home of all the rulers of Florence until 1828. The Pitti Palace was expanded extensively during the 16th century; one of its main architects was Ammannati, who built the imposing courtyard at the core of the palace looking out to the Giardino di Boboli (Boboli Gardens) behind.

The front of the palace faces on to a naked piazza without shade or seats.

The palace, like all Florentine museums, is subject to sudden unannounced closures. Lacking any guidance through its complex layout, the Pitti is the most unfriendly, and the most expensive, of Florence's museums.

At the same time it is one of the most important. The Medici collected art objects with an almost manic determination, although, as time went on, with diminishing selectivity. Many of the objects they collected remain in the palace, which is divided into no fewer than six museums and art galleries. The picture collection housed in the Galleria Palatina (Palatine Gallery) is second in importance only to the Uffizi. The palace has, however, been deliberately left as a family home. Church services are still held in the Palatine Chapel in the great courtyard and the paintings in the palace itself are displayed exactly as they were originally hung. The opulent rooms are exhibits in their own right and the overall effect is rich but confusing. Altogether, it is advisable to allow several hours for a visit. A separate admission ticket is necessary for each museum or gallery.

Galleria Palatina

This is the palace's main display area, access to which is up the vast ceremonial staircase designed by Ammannati. Although there are at least 26 rooms in the Palatine Gallery, the most important paintings are displayed in the five great state rooms which overlook the Piazza del Pitti. The ceiling of each room is decorated with frescos whose classical subjects have given their names to the rooms: the Sala di Venere (Venus Room) and the Sala di Apollo both have paintings by Titian; the Sala di Marte (Mars) has works by Rubens and Tintoretto; the Sala di Giove (Jove) and the Sala di Saturna (Saturn) both have superb works by Raphael. The Sala di Giove (Jupiter) also served as the Medici throne room. The Sala dell'Iliade was painted as late as the 19th century with subjects from Homer's epic poem.

Galleria d'Arte Moderna

Despite its name, the Modern Art Gallery consists mostly of 19th-century paintings. There are a number of lively historic battle scenes, but also some highly evocative paintings of Tuscan rural life painted in the early decades of the 20th century.

Museo degli Argenti

The Silverware Museum is situated on the ground floor (access from the courtyard) and contains a far greater range of exhibits than its name implies. Among the objects on display are the wonderful antique vases collected by Lorenzo the Magnificent – who could not resist the temptation to have his name engraved upon them.

Galleria del Costume

Situated in a pavilion in the southern wing of the palace (entered from the Boboli Gardens), this gallery is used for changing displays of court and theatrical costume dating from the 18th century up to the 1930s.

Piazza del Pitti (tel: Galleria Palatina 055 210 323; Museo degli Argenti 212 557; Galleria d'Arte Moderna 287 096; Galleria del Costume 212 557). All museums open: Tuesday to Saturday, 9am–2pm; Sunday, 9am–1pm. Closed Monday. Separate admission charge for each museum. Nearby: Boboli Gardens.

Inside the Galleria Palatina

PALAZZO VECCHIO (OLD PALACE)

This grim but imposing building has been the seat of Florentine government for nearly 700 years, from 1299 when the palace was finished right down to the present day. In the soaring, majestic tower hung the great bell, called *la Vacca* (the Cow), whose bellowing once summoned the citizens at times of danger. Today, it is still the town hall, though much of the day-to-day business of local government has been transferred to modern buildings located on the outskirts of the city.

The entrance courtyard was designed by Michelozzo in 1444. Cosimo I's court architect, Giorgio Vasari, added

Above and left: the Palazzo Vecchio

the stucco columns and the charming frescos, depicting Austrian cities, to welcome Joanna of Austria, the bride of Cosimo's eldest son, Francesco. The enchanting little fountain of a laughing child holding a dolphin is a 16th-century copy of Verrochio's *Puttino*. The original can be seen in one of the rooms upstairs.

Beyond the entrance courtyard, stairs to the right lead up to the Apartementi Monumentale (State Apartments). The first of these is the Salone dei Cinquecento (the Room of the Five Hundred). Here the republican Consiglio Maggiore (Great Council) used to meet after the expulsion of the Medici. Michelangelo and Leonardo da Vinci were both commissioned to decorate it but neither of them got beyond the preliminary stages. The room was used as the Italian Parliament for the brief period when Florence was the capital of Italy from 1865 to 1870. The present frescos are the work of

Vasari and exalt the military triumphs of Cosimo I. Particularly interesting is the Siege of Florence, which provides a picture of the appearance of Florence in the mid-16th century.

Just off this large room is the smaller Studiolo di Francesco I. Vasari designed this rather claustrophobic study for the scholarly but introverted eldest son of Cosimo I. Francesco was greatly interested in alchemy and the natural sciences and the decorations reflect these interests. The crowded pictures and statues form a miniature gallery of Florentine Mannerist art. Among them are portraits of Francesco's parents, Cosimo I and Eleanora of Toledo, painted by Bronzino.

Next comes the Quartiere di Leone X. Leo X was the first Medici pope and the decoration of this series of rooms, by Vasari and Bronzino, is unabashed propaganda for the family.

Of the remaining rooms, the Sala dei Gigli (Room of the Lilies) is the most splendid. The lily (or fleur-de-lis), one of the symbols of Florence, appears all over the walls of this room. Donatello's statue of *Judith and Holofernes* is also displayed here; the statue was made as a warning to tyrants, as the carvings on its base indicate. The statue stood outside, in the Piazza della Signoria, before being restored and brought here. Just off this

The beautiful entrance courtyard with its child and dolphin fountain

room is the Cancelleria, the office used by Niccolo Machiavelli during his period of office as secretary to the Republic. It contains his 16th-century bust.

Another room that is occasionally open is the notorious L'Alberghettino, 'the little hotel'. This room in the tower was used as a prison. Cosimo de'Medici and Savonarola were both imprisoned here at various times.

Piazza della Signoria (tel: 055 27681).
Open: Monday to Friday, 9am–7pm;
Sunday 8am–1pm. Closed Saturday.
Admission charge. Nearby: Bargello

NICCOLO MACHIAVELLI (1469–1527)

Machiavelli's name has entered most European languages as a synonym for all that is deceitful and devious. This use of his name is based on his treatise, *The Prince*, in which he described the mechanics of tyranny. In reality he was a most unfortunate man. He was tortured on the rack by the Medici for being a suspect republican, but he was later dismissed from office by the republicans because of his reluctant service to the Medici. Though *The Prince* is his best-known work, he also wrote a number of plays and essays in what the Italian journalist, Luigi Barzini, describes as 'the most beautiful, lean and muscular prose'.

Piazza della Signoria

*F*or all their artistic genius, the Florentines never learned how to build a decent public square. With the exception of the Piazza Santissima Annunziata, the city's main squares are unremarkable. The cathedral is crowded into the small and shapeless Piazza del Duomo; the Piazza del Pitti is a dreary asphalt waste and the Piazza della Signoria was never planned. This last square stands at the very heart of the city. Excavations carried out in the 1980s revealed extensive Roman and Etruscan remains beneath the square and the Palazzo Vecchio partly stands on the site of the Roman theatre.

The citizens of Florence assembled in this square when summoned by the great bell of the Palazzo Vecchio. The square was thus their parliament. Here, too, they welcomed important visitors and punished political enemies (a tablet set approximately in the centre of the piazza marks the site of the execution of Savonarola). Despite this importance, the piazza has no particular shape,

unlike the majestic harmony of Siena's main square, the Campo. In fact the square consists of nothing but a haphazard collection of buildings. It has been like that for over 400 years; a contemporary painting of the execution of Savonarola, which took place in the piazza in 1498, shows it looking almost exactly as it does today. Cosimo I commissioned Michelangelo to build a loggia all the way round to provide a degree of unity, but he never got down to the job. Florentines today just like it the way it is.

Fronting the Palazzo Vecchio is the *arringhiera*, the platform from which members of the city council once addressed the citizens. To the right is a copy of Michelangelo's *David*, a copy of Donatello's *Judith and Holofernes* and a copy of the same sculptor's *Marzocco*, the heraldic lion of the city.

A short step away from these monumental sculptures is the Loggia dei Lanzi, so called because the German lancers who form the bodyguard of Cosimo I had their barracks near here. The loggia was built between 1376 and 1382 and forms a graceful porch, even though (whether by accident or design)

Ammannati's dramatic Neptune fountain, nicknamed 'Big Whitey'

Giambologna's equestrian statue of Grand Duke Cosimo I

nearly all the statues placed here depict violent action.

Predominant among them is Cellini's *Perseus trampling Medusa*; one of the finest of late Renaissance sculptures (1545), it is also one of the most heartless. Cellini portrays Medusa not as a monster but as a beautiful naked woman – which makes it all the more shocking to see black blood pouring from her severed trunk while Perseus, a handsome youth, complacently holds up the severed head. In his autobiography Cellini describes how he ran out of metal while casting the statue and frantically threw in all the household pewter.

Also in the loggia is Giambologna's *Rape of the Sabines* (1583) and his *Hercules Fighting the Centaur Nessus* (1599) together with Pio Fedi's continuance of the tradition into the 19th century, the *Rape of Polixena* (1866).

To the left of the Palazzo Vecchio's façade is the Neptune Fountain, an enormous, and frequently dry monster, by Ammannati (1575). It had barely been completed before it was nicknamed *Il Biancone* (Big Whitey) and a mocking verse circulated describing how Ammannati had wasted so much good stone.

Further out in the square is the equestrian statue of Duke Cosimo I. Giambologna worked at this symbol of ducal power for over 12 years, from 1587 to 1599. The panels in the pedestal show Cosimo's conquest of Siena and Pope Pius V bestowing the title of Grand Duke of Tuscany upon him.

PONTE SANTA TRINITA

The fact that the Arno runs from east to west through Florence condemned its beautiful bridges towards the end of World War II. The Germans used the river as a defensive line during their northward retreat and all the city's bridges, with the exception of the Ponte Vecchio, were blown up. All these bridges have since been rebuilt exactly as they were before 1944.

Ponte Santa Trinità is the most important of the bridges of Florence both in terms of its siting and because it was deliberately designed as a work of art. The bridge was built (or rather rebuilt, since a bridge had stood here since 1252) on the orders of Cosimo I. The design is attributed to Michelangelo, who is said to have sketched out the subtle, elliptical curve of the arches. Ammannati carried out the actual construction work between 1567 and 1569. Cosimo I did not simply want a bridge across the river linking the two halves of his city; he demanded that the land be raised on both embankments to provide a grand sweeping approach.

After the bridge was blown up in 1944 there was a great deal of debate about how the bridge was to be rebuilt. There was even a suggestion that it should be cast in ferro-concrete but eventually the decision was taken to copy the original plans exactly. Demolished blocks of stone were salvaged from the bed of the river and the quarry in the Boboli Gardens, which had supplied the original stone, was reworked to supply any blocks that were missing. When the bridge was reopened in 1957 it was complete – all except for the head of *Spring*, one of the statues of the Four Seasons which decorate the two ends of the bridge. The head was finally found in the river in 1961 and ceremonially displayed on a velvet cushion in the Palazzo Vecchio before it was finally rejoined to the body.

PONTE VECCHIO (OLD BRIDGE)

The oldest of all Florence's bridges was spared destruction in 1944 because of the intervention of the wartime German consul, Gerhard Wolf. Spanning the narrowest section of the river, this bridge almost certainly stands on the site of the first Roman bridge. The Ponte Vecchio was built in 1345 to replace an earlier wooden bridge that had been washed away by one of the savage floods to which the Arno is subject. It is one of the last surviving bridges in Europe with houses and shops built along it. Tanners were the first to build workshops on the bridge, using the river to soak their hides. Butchers and blacksmiths also had premises on the bridge but they

THE FLOOD OF 1966

The Florentines have little love for their river; Dante referred to it as 'the accursed ditch'. For much of the year the Arno lies low in its channel but the height of the embankments shows only too clearly how high the river can rise. There have been at least four major floods before the disaster of November 1966. Although there was ample warning, the moment when the banks finally broke occurred with such suddenness that all the people in the railway underpass, some distance from the river, were drowned. Thirty-five people died altogether and untold numbers of works of art were damaged – so many that restoration is still in process.

were all evicted in 1593 on the orders of Ferdinando I who objected to the smell, noise and mess made by these trades. Goldsmiths then took over the cramped workshops, and they have been there ever since. Today the Ponte Vecchio is the most popular tourist spot in the city, and on the route of the evening *passeggiata*.

SPEDALE DEGLI INNOCENTI (FOUNDLING HOSPITAL)

Founded in 1419, this was Europe's first orphanage and it still operates as such. Brunelleschi was commissioned to build the hospital and the delicate colonnade fronting the orphanage was completed in 1426. The beautiful ceramic plaques of swaddled babies, set in the spandrels, are the work of Andrea della Robbia and

Right: the Innocenti orphanage
Below: the Ponte Vecchio

were added in 1487. The gallery inside the orphanage contains a number of fine Renaissance paintings donated by benefactors, including Ghirlandaio's splendid *Adoration of the Magi*.
Piazza SantissimaAnnunziata 12 (tel: 055 243 670). Open: Monday, Tuesday and Thursday to Saturday, 8.30am–2pm; Sunday, 8.30am–1pm. Admission charge. Nearby: Museo Archeologico.

Uffizi, Galleria Degli (Uffizi Gallery)

*T*he building was designed by Vasari in 1560 as a suite of administrative offices (*uffizi*) for Cosimo I. Construction continued until 1586 and the gallery encloses three sides of what was once a street leading from Piazza della Signoria down to the river. Cosimo's heirs, most notably Francesco I, decided to display their ever-expanding collection in the 'offices' and in 1743 Anna Maria Lodovica, the last of the Medici, bequeathed the collection and the building to the people of Florence. Successors to the Medici continued to add to the Uffizi collection and works are still being acquired. In the reception area, for instance, there is a startlingly modern work, *The Battle of San Martino*, by Carrado Caylis (1936).

Today the gallery contains the world's greatest collection of Florentine Renaissance paintings, covering the whole history of the period. It also possesses a rich variety of works from other countries and periods – it has, for instance, some important works by Rembrandt. Other galleries may have a larger number of paintings, but few other galleries have so many world-famous works of art that simply demand to be looked at.

Queueing for the Uffizi

The risk of suffering from mental indigestion is a hazard throughout Italy, higher still in Florence and virtually unavoidable in the Uffizi unless you are selective. The best survival technique is to choose a dozen or so paintings or sculptures (assisted by the guidebook obtainable in the reception area) for detailed study and resist the rest.

Despite the fact that the entrance fee makes this one of the most expensive galleries in Italy, there is always a queue at the entrance during the high tourist season, so you should arrive early in the day and allow at least half an hour to gain admission. Most of the gallery is on the third floor; access is by means of Vasari's monumental staircase (there is a lift for disabled visitors). There is an informal one-way system in operation through the gallery and in the high season it is virtually impossible to retrace your steps in order to have another look because of the crowds. Fortunately, the gallery no longer closes at lunchtime and you can stay all day if you have the stamina.

In May 1993, a car bomb exploded at the back of the west wing of the Uffizi. Although the building's structure remained sound, three paintings were destroyed and some 30 others damaged. The museum's most important works, however, survived untouched.

HIGHLIGHTS OF THE UFFIZI
Reception area
This area has frescos of famous Florentines by Andrea del Castagno (1421–57), including portraits of Dante and Boccaccio which, though painted posthumously, are based on contemporary portraits and are widely accepted as faithful likenesses.

Rooms 2 and 3
Here you can trace the dawning of the Renaissance through three examples of a *Maestà* (the word means Majesty, and paintings of this type show the Virgin enthroned in heaven surrounded by saints); they are by Cimabue (1240–1302), Duccio di Buoninsegna (*c*1260–1320) and Giotto (1266–1337). Another powerful work is the *Annunciation* by Simone Martini (*c*1284–1344), all a blaze of gold. The subjects are still formally presented but the Madonna is shown as human, and there are glimpses of everyday life in the costumes and buildings depicted.

Room 7
Here are two superb portraits by Piero della Francesca (*c*1420–92): *Federico da Montefeltro* and his wife *Battista Sforza*. Montefeltro, the Duke of Urbino, was one of the first princes to espouse Renaissance and Humanist values at his court. Near by is *The Battle of San Romano* by Paolo Uccello (1396–1475), essentially an exercise in the new-found technique of perspective. This is one of three paintings Uccello made on the same subject.

The Palazzo Vecchio tower framed by the Uffizi's arcades

Rooms 8 and 9
Filippo Lippi (1406–69) was, according to Vasari, a rascally drunken protégé of the Medici, but he produced ethereal Madonnas, often using his mistress as his model. Here are two fine examples, the *Madonna with Angels* and the *Coronation of the Virgin*. Antonio del Pollaiuolo (*c*1432–98) dissected corpses to learn about human anatomy, applying the results of his study to paintings as in the two tiny *Labours of Hercules*.

Mysterious and compelling: Botticelli's *Birth of Venus* and *Primavera*

Rooms 10–14

The works of Sandro Botticelli (c1445–1510) displayed in these rooms are probably the Uffizi's most powerful attractions. In his early life as a protégé of the Medici, Botticelli was obsessed by mythology and the works he painted at this time include the enchanting *Birth of Venus* and the mysterious *Primavera* (Spring); the same beautiful model appears in both pictures as Venus and as the enigmatically smiling goddess Flora. Later in life, Botticelli fell under the influence of Savonarola and devoted himself to religious subjects; typical of this phase is the *Adoration of the Magi* in which Botticelli included portraits of the Medici and a self-portrait (he is the figure on the right in a saffron robe looking out of the picture at the viewer).

By total contrast, this room also contains the *Adoration of the Shepherds* by the Flemish painter, Hugo van der Goes, painted around 1475. The shepherds in this picture are realistic, manual workers and not, as in

Botticelli's painting, posing courtiers.

Room 15

This room contains a painting by Andrea Verrocchio (c1435–88), the *Baptism of Christ*. Verrocchio's apprentice was Leonardo da Vinci (1452–1519), who painted the angel on the left of the picture and may have painted most of the *Annunciation* in the same room. Near by hangs Leonardo's unfinished *Adoration of the Magi*.

Room 18

This octagonal room, called the Tribuna, is itself an exhibit. Designed in 1584 to hold the most important Medici possessions, the dome is inlaid with mother-of-pearl and the floor is made of a semi-precious marble inlay. Among the treasures displayed here are the *Medici Venus* (a 2nd-century BC Roman copy of a Greek 4th-century original) and other antique sculptures, including the delightful *Dancing Faun*. Also on display are court portraits of the Medici family, among them posthumous portraits of *Cosimo II Vecchio* by Jacopo Pontormo (1494–1556) and *Lorenzo the Magnificent* by Giorgio Vasari (1511–74).

Room 20

The Medici's wide-ranging taste is well illustrated by the works of German painters hung in this room. Albrecht Dürer (1471–1528) is represented by the portrait of his father, Lucas Cranach (1472–1553) by his *Adam and Eve* and (rather oddly for a family, one of whose number, Pope Leo X excommunicated Luther) his *Portrait of Martin Luther*. It is interesting to compare this picture with the School of Holbein portrait of the English statesman and martyr, Sir Thomas More, in room 22.

Room 25

Michelangelo Buonarroti (1475–1564) is represented here by the stunning *Holy Family*, the only one of his paintings to survive in Florence but one that was enormously influential on the Mannerist artists of the High Renaissance, because of its adventurous use of colour and the unusual pose of the Virgin.

Room 26

This room contains a major work by Raphael (1483–1520), his portrait of the Medici Pope Leo X. The short-sighted pope is shownstudying a richly illuminated manuscript while his half-brother, Cardinal Giulio de'Medici (later Pope Clement VII), and Cardinal Luigi de Rossi stand deferentially by him.

Room 28

This contains Titian's sensual and intimate *Venus of Urbino* (1538).

Corridoio Vasariano (Vasari's Corridor)

After Cosimo I moved across the river to the Pitti Palace, he wanted to be able to walk back and forth between his home and the city centre discreetly – and in safety. From this developed one of the most extraordinary structures in Florence. Vasari built a corridor which, leaving the southeastern corner of the Uffizi, runs on arches high above the pavement along the embankment as far as the Ponte Vecchio; it then soars over the top of the bridge, passes in front of the church of Santa Felicita and eventually links up with the Pitti Palace. The corridor is used to display a remarkable collection of artists' self-portraits. In order to visit the Corridor it is necessary to book beforehand at the Uffizi ticket office or telephone.
Piazzale degli Uffizi 6 (tel: 055 218 341). Open Tuesday to Saturday, 9am–7pm; Sunday, 9am–1pm. Closed Monday. Admission charge. Nearby: Palazzo Vecchio.

Ancient Roman and Greek sculptures line the Uffizi's main corridor

THREE GREAT ARTISTS

LEONARDO DA VINCI
(1452–1519)

Leonardo was born in the village of Vinci, the illegitimate son of a Florentine lawyer. His career as a painter serves as a link between the age of the old-fashioned *bottega* (workshop), when the artist was regarded simply as a craftsman, and the High Renaissance, when the artist was courted by princes. One of the paintings on which he worked as a *bottega* apprentice is Verrocchio's *Baptism of Christ*, now hung in room 15 of the Uffizi (see page 64). Leonardo had a highly analytical mind; in the modern world, perhaps, he might have been a great scientist or engineer. His notebooks are crammed with ideas for new machines including a helicopter and a tank. Painting was only one of his skills and many of these were left unfinished as his mind leapt on to another subject. He died in France where he had been staying as the guest of the king, François I.

The inventions of Leonardo da Vinci

Cellini's bronze of *Perseus with the head of Medusa*, in the Loggia dei Lanzi, Piazza della Signoria

MICHELANGELO BUONARROTI
(1475–1564)

Michelangelo also trained in a *bottega*, serving very briefly as an apprentice in Ghirlandaio's workshop. At an early age he benefited from Medici patronage for, at the age of 13, he entered the school of art set up by Lorenzo de'Medici. His greatest work of art is in Rome where, under pressure from Pope Julius II, he painted the ceiling of the Sistine Chapel. Nevertheless he regarded himself primarily as a sculptor. Unlike Leonardo he was also involved in politics, a passionate republican who fought for the defence of Florence against his Medici patrons during the siege of

Left: Michelangelo's *David*
Above: Michelangelo's tomb in Santa Croce

1530. During that siege he was put in charge of defensive works and supervised the extension of the city walls to embrace the hill and church of San Miniato (see page 75).

BENVENUTO CELLINI
(1500–71)

Apart from his exquisite sculptures, Cellini is best known for the remarkable *Autobiography* in which he recounted his swashbuckling life in boastful detail, including his claims to have killed scores of people as a gunner during the 1527 siege of Rome, going about this slaughter safe in the knowledge that the Pope had absolved him beforehand 'for any murders I might commit'. His most famous work is the *Perseus* in Florence (see page 31) but, in his capacity as a goldsmith, he also created a remarkable salt cellar for François I of France. His death approximately coincides with the end of the Italian Renaissance.

Days Out From Florence

FIESOLE

High on its hill, barely 15 minutes by bus from the city centre, Florence's old enemy is now its playground. Founded by the Etruscans and then developed by the Romans, Fiesole was the first city to be conquered by Florence. In the heat of summer it is a delightfully refreshing place, much appreciated by Florentines and visitors alike. Its most popular feature is the great Roman theatre. Tucked into the side of the hill, its grass-covered ruins and shady corners make it a pleasant spot for a picnic – and the adjoining museum adds interest. The monastery of San Francesco, with its exquisite little cloister, stands to the

west of the main square, on the site of an Etruscan temple, and provides superb views over Florence.

Location: 8km north of Florence. Getting there: Bus 7 from Florence. Roman Theatre (tel: 59477). Open: summer, 9am–7pm; winter, 10am–4pm. Closed Tuesday. Admission charge.

PISTOIA

Pistoia is the capital of Tuscany's smallest province and it tends to be overlooked on the tourist circuit because the historic core is surrounded by ugly industrial suburbs. In compensation is the fact that much of the core of the city, within the 14th-century walls, is largely

FIESOLE

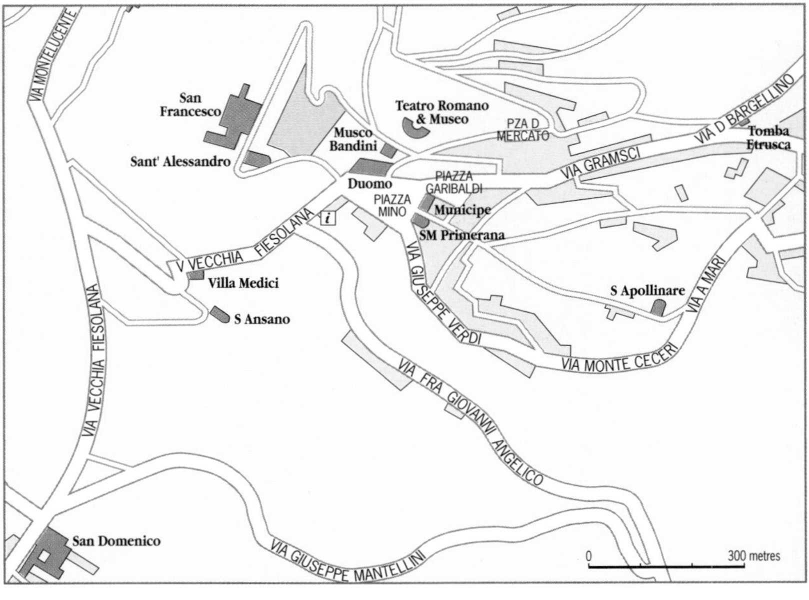

In Prato's main square, the splendid Piazza del Duomo

unspoiled. The enormous Piazza del Duomo is the heart of the city. Although it seems thrown together, rather than planned, the great buildings around it harmonise in a curious manner. They include the 12th-century green and white striped Duomo (Cathedral), the 14th-century Baptistery and the Palazzo della Podesta of the same date. The late 13th-century Palazzo Comunale houses the city art gallery whose exhibits include striking bronze sculptures by the abstract artist, Marino Marini, born in this city in 1901. The façade of the Ospedale del Ceppo, behind the Palazzo Comunale, bears a famous glazed terracotta frieze from the workshops of Giovanni della Robbia.

Location: 37km west of Florence. Getting there: trains run regularly from Florence. Tourist Office: Piazza del Duomo (tel: 0573 21622). Galleria Communale open: Tuesday to Saturday, 9am–1pm and 3pm–7pm; Sunday 9am–12.30pm. Closed Monday. Admission charge.

PRATO

One of the most revealing accounts of life in medieval Italy is Iris Origo's biography of *The Merchant of Prato*. Based on the voluminous archives of the wealthy wool merchant, Francesco Datini, it gives us an intimate picture of social, commercial and political life in the 14th century. Five hundred years later, cloth is still Prato's major industry.

Inside its girdling walls, the old city remains largely intact, however, inviting the visitor to stroll at leisure. Look out for Datini's palace (the Palazzo Datini) on Via Rinaldesca. The offices of the charity which he founded in 1410 are still located on the first floor and the front of the palace is frescoed with scenes from his life. Near by, in Piazza del Commune, there is a statue of Datini and the city's art gallery, housed in the Palazzo Pretorio. At the heart of the city is the Duomo (Cathedral) with its pulpit located on the outside wall of the church, carved by Donatello and used to display the miraculous Girdle of the Virgin on ceremonial occasions. Inside the cathedral you can see Filippo Lippi's frescos on the *Death of St John the Baptist*. If you have time, do not miss the great Castello dell'Imperatore, built in the 13th century for the Emperor Frederick II. Although the castle is empty, its wall walks provide a panorama of the city.

Location: 19km west of Florence. Getting there: trains run regularly from Florence. Tourist Office: Via Cairoll 48 (tel: 0574 24112). Open: Monday to Saturday, 8.30am–1.30pm and 4pm–7pm. Closed Sunday.
Castello dell'Imperatore. Open: Wednesday to Monday, 9.30am–12.30pm and 3pm–6.30pm. Closed Tuesday.
Galleria Communale. Open: Monday, and Wednesday to Saturday, 9am–12.30pm and 3pm–6.30pm; Sunday, 9.30am–12.30pm. Closed Tuesday. Admission charge.

Florence South to North

This walk will take you from the Porta Romana, the southernmost gate of the city, up to the cathedral, passing through streets lined with little shops and workshops. Expect to encounter heavy traffic on the first part of the walk, up to the Via Sant'Agostino junction (for that reason, avoid doing the walk at rush hour or with children). *Allow 1 hour.*
Begin at the Porta Romana.

1 PORTA ROMANA

Florence lost a substantial part of its walls and gates when it

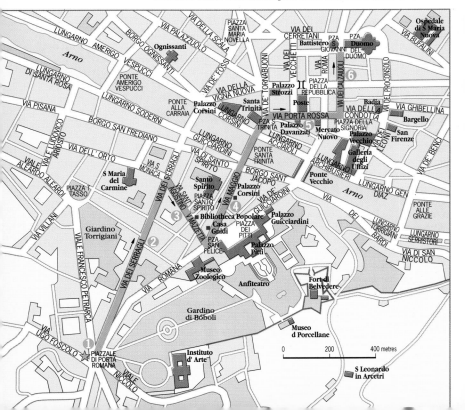

became the temporary capital of Italy in the 1860s. The enormous Porta Romana (Rome Gate) still has its vast doors, nearly 6m high, *in situ*. The gate also served as a barracks and custom post. The 14th-century Florentine, Franco Sachetti, tells the story of how a farmer tried to smuggle eggs hidden in his trousers through the Porta Romana. A rival informed the customs officer on duty who firmly but courteously insisted that the farmer be seated.

Proceed down Via de'Serragli, past the Giardino Torrigiani, a private park.

2 VIA DE'SERRAGLI

All along this road, which runs like an arrow into the heart of the city, there are innumerable little workshops, groceries and the like. On the right is the Cinema Goldoni where a plaque records that Edward Gordon Craig founded a theatre workshop here in 1913.

Turn right at the junction with Via Sant'Agostino (on the corner is a take-away pizza bakery where you can stock up for a picnic). Continue on to Piazza Santo Spirito.

3 PIAZZA SANTO SPIRITO

The square is pleasantly Bohemian with a market and lots of little cafés and shops. The church of Santo Spirito is the work of Brunellschi and well worth a visit (see page 45).

Carry on down Via Mazzetta to Piazza San Felice, with its enormous column, and turn left up Via Maggio (if you want to go on to the Boboli Gardens carry on past the Pitti Palace on the right).

4 VIA MAGGIO

The earlier name of Via Maggio was Via Maggiore (Main Street) which better describes its importance. On each side

are palaces built from the 15th century onwards. The first on the right (Piazza San Felice 8) is the Casa Guidi, former home of the poets Robert and Elizabeth Barrett Browning.

Cross the river using Ponte Santa Trinità (see page 60) and continue into Piazza Santa Trinità (see page 45). Immediately ahead is Via de'Tornabuoni with its fashionable (and highly expensive) shops. Turn right along Via Porta Rossa. Careful navigation is needed here for you are in the very heart of medieval Florence, with its tangle of narrow streets. Continue past the Palazzo Davanzati, on the right (see page 50) until you reach the Mercato Nuovo, also on the right.

5 MERCATO NUOVO

The Mercato Nuovo is the goal of all visitors because of the small bronze fountain on the southern side called *Il Porcellino* (the Little Boar) which dates to 1612; the snout is polished gold from the custom that whoever rubs it will return to Florence. The loggia behind (built in the 1500s despite its name, meaning 'New Market') is filled with souvenir stalls.

Continue down Via Porta Rossa and turn left into Via de'Calzaiuoli.

6 VIA DE'CALZAIUOLI

It is typical of Florence that this lively street, the true 'High Street' of the city, does not have a grand name but is simply called the 'Street of the Hosiers'. Everyone comes here to shop and stroll after work. At night in summer it is also the haunt of numerous buskers, including fortune-tellers, jugglers, musicians and mime artists.

Continue up the street to reach Piazza del Duomo with the Baptistery to the left and the Duomo (Cathedral) to the right.

Lucca
Pisa Firenze
Arezzo
Siena
Grosseto

Florence
West to East

This semi-circular route covers a number of interesting sights in the north of the city not normally seen by visitors. *Allow 1 ½ hours.*
Begin at the main railway station, Santa Maria Novella.

1 STAZIONE CENTRALE DI SANTA MARIA NOVELLA

Fascist Italy built some good railway stations and this one, built in 1933, is an excellent example with a clear and logical layout inside. This ceases outside where pedestrians and traffic battle for space in an absurdly designed forecourt. The great church of Santa Maria Novella (see page 44) stands opposite turning its back on the station.

Take the underpass from in front of the station into Piazza dell'Unità Italiana and from there walk up Via Sant'Antonino, a

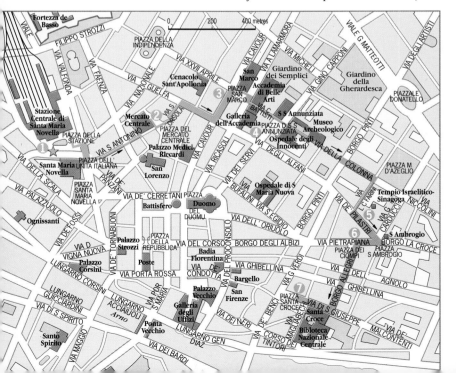

*delightful and lively little street, full of small
bars and friendly shops. Take the second
left, Via dell'Ariento, which will be full of
market stalls on most days. Walk through
the stalls and look for the Mercato Centrale
on the right.*

2 MERCATO CENTRALE

This vast covered food market has
numerous cafés, cooked-food stalls and
a *tavola calda* canteen, much used by
local workers, where you can chose
yourself a three-course meal with wine
for about L6,000 – but get there by
noon for it seems that everybody else in
the quarter wants to eat there.
*Exit the market by the back doors on to
Piazza del Mercato Centrale and head
towards Via Rosina. Turn left into Via
Taddea and immediately right into Via S
Orsola. Turn right again along Via Guelfa
then left along Via Cavour, one of the city's
main traffic arteries. Continue up to Piazza
San Marco.*

3 PIAZZA SAN MARCO

This square stands in the heart of the
university district and is invariably full of
young people during term time. Ahead
is San Marco convent (see page 51).
*Cross Piazza San Marco, bearing right to
exit past the Accademia di Belle Arti (see
page 26), walking down Via C Battisti.*

4 PIAZZA DELLA SANTISSIMA
ANNUNZIATA

This brings you to one of Florence's
very few planned Renaissance squares,
the beautiful Piazza della Santissima
Annunziata, with its two grotesque
fountains in the centre, and the spendid
colonnade of the Ospedale degli
Innocenti to the west (see page 61).
*Exit through the arch alongside Innocenti
which leads into Via della Colonna, and*

*watch out for traffic. The pavements along
this street are narrow or non-existent and
the traffic is fast. At Piazza M d'Azeglio
turn right into Via L C Farini to the
Tempio Israelitico (Synagogue).*

5 TEMPIO ISRAELITICO

Jews have had mixed fortunes in
Florence: frequently welcomed and
frequently expelled. The Synagogue,
built in 1874, has a small museum on
the first floor illustrating the history of
Florentine Jewry. (Open: Monday to
Thursday, 11am–1pm and 2pm–5pm;
Friday and Sunday, 10am–1pm.)
*Continue down Via L C Farini, then turn
left in Via de'Pilastri to Piazza
Sant'Ambrogio. Turn right in this little
square, down Via Pietrapiana, to reach the
Piazza dei Ciompi on the left.*

6 PIAZZA DEI CIOMPI

The Ciompi were the lowest level of
Florentine cloth workers whose rebellion
against the nobles in the 14th century
was one of the important steps towards
republicanism. Vasari built the Loggia
del Pesce which stands to one side of the
square; an unusually elegant classical
arcade that once served as a fish market.
Today the piazza is the site of a flea
market where you might like to browse,
even though you are unlikely to pick up
anything of real value.
*Leave the square by following Borgo Allegri
southwards, heading for the enormous bulk
of Santa Croce (see page 38), then turn
right along Via di S Giuseppe to enter
Piazza Santa Croce.*

7 PIAZZA SANTA CROCE

Surrounded by medieval buildings, this
is still very much the centre of a living
community where local artists display
their work for sale.

Rural Florence

This will take you, in a matter of minutes, from the hurly burly of the Ponte Vecchio to the tranquillity of olive groves and gardens. The walk is ideal for children, though there are some steep streets and flights of steps to climb. *Allow 2 hours.*

Leave the Ponte Vecchio at its southern end and take the second left into Piazza Santa Felicita. Leave the piazza by the steep, narrow and winding lane to the right of the church façade, the Costa di San Giorgio. About half way up you will pass number 19, on the right, where the famous astronomer, Galileo, once lived.

Turn right at the junction with Via del Forte di San Giorgio to approach one of Florence's hidden delights, the Forte di Belvedere.

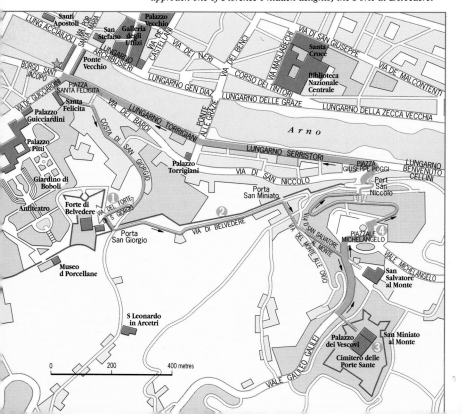

1 FORTE DI BELVEDERE

Also known as the Forte di San Giorgio, this huge fortress was built by the Medici in 1590 – not to protect the citizens but to overawe them. The gun ports point *towards* the city! Open daily (9am–8pm, admission free) the fortress provides a superb vantage point from which to view Florence.

On leaving the fort, turn immediately right and then left at the junction into the Via di Belvedere.

2 VIA DI BELVEDERE

This well-named lane (literally 'Good View Road') runs along the foot of the mighty city wall, built in the 13th century and heightened in the 16th. To the right you will catch glimpses of olive groves descending steeply into the valley while high up in the distance is the gleaming marble front of San Miniato al Monte, your ultimate destination.

Descend the steep lane to reach Porta San Miniato. Turn right here towards Via del Monte alle Croci and, after a short climb, look for a steep flight of steps on the left, called Via del San Savatore al Monte. At the top of the steps turn right in the wide Viale Galileo Galilei and, after a short distance, cross the road to ascend the great monumental flight of steps that leads up to the church of San Miniato al Monte (open daily, 8.30am–6pm in summer, to 5pm in winter).

3 SAN MINIATO AL MONTE

Begun in 1015, this is one of the most splendid Romanesque churches in Tuscany; it is also the second oldest in Florence after the much-loved Baptistery. The dramatic green, black and white marble front of San Miniato was begun in 1090 and paid for by the Arte di Calimala, the wealthy Guild of

Cloth Importers (the Guild's emblem, an eagle holding a bale of cloth in its talons, crowns the roof). The solemn, majestic interior is almost entirely unchanged since it was built. The marble pavement, inlaid with the signs of the Zodiac and animals and birds, dates from 1207. Surrounding the church is a cemetery full of remarkable monuments. Among others, the painter Annigoni (1910–88) lies buried here. (Open: summer, 8am–noon and 2pm–7pm; winter, 8am–noon and 2pm–6pm; Sunday, 2.30–7pm.)

Retrace your steps along Viale Galileo Galilei, and so enter Piazzale Michelangelo.

Fine views from Piazzale Michelangelo

4 PIAZZALE MICHELANGELO

This elevated square, high above the Arno, provides the most famous view of Florence, but it is an uncomfortable spot with its roaring traffic, parked coaches and souvenir stalls.

To return to central Florence, look for a short flight of steps to the left of the piazzale and follow this to a series of footpaths which lead down through the dramatically landscaped hillside. The paths will take you down to the Lungarno Serristori, running alongside the river. Turn left here and a ten-minute walk will take you back to the Ponte Vecchio.

Fiesole to Settignano

This 6km rural walk will take you, through woods and open countryside, from one exquisite little hilltop town to another. During the first part of the walk, along the narrow and winding main road, watch out for traffic. You would be wise to take refreshments with you, for there are no shops or cafés along the route. *Allow 2 hours.*

The No 7 bus will take you to Fiesole from central Florence. At the terminus in Fiesole, on Piazzo Mino, head eastwards (uphill and away from the cathedral) towards the bronze equestrian statue of Vittorio Emanuele II meeting Garibaldi (1906), which stands in front of the town hall (Palazzo Pretorio) decorated with ancient coats of arms. From here, walk leftwards into Piazza Garibaldi and from there down Via Gramsci, following the signposts to Vincigliata.

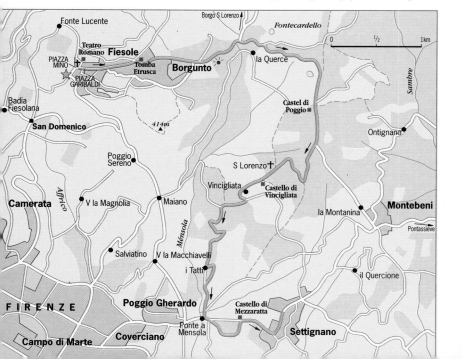

ETRUSCAN TOMBS

A few hundred metres further along a sign indicates the existence of Etruscan tombs (Tomba Etrusca) down the lane on the left. They are only a short distance away and well worth a visit, two massive structures set in a little green garden and all the more attractive in that they are just taken for granted.
Retrace your steps back to the main road and continue on.

VIEWPOINT

About a kilometre further along is a spectacular view back to the Roman amphitheatre at Fiesole, over the olive groves stretching down into the valley. _The road now enters a pine forest. The countryside here is curiously empty for such a densely populated region. It is difficult to believe that, at almost any point, a bus could take you back to Florence within the space of a few minutes. At the next T-junction take the well-signposted road to Settignano/Vincigliata and continue through the wood._

CASTLES

Little traffic comes down this country road so you can now relax and enjoy the superb scenery. On the right you will see the Castel di Poggio clinging to an escarpment. At the junction beyond take the road to Vincigliata. You now enter an open country of vineyards and olive groves. About half-way down the hill is the Castello di Vincigliata, first built in 1031 and sacked by English mercenaries in the 14th century. John Temple Leader, an English Member of Parliament, restored the castle in 1855. On the wall facing the road a series of plaques announce the names of the notables who visited him here, including Princess Beatrice, the daughter of Queen Victoria. The castle is not open to the public.
Continue on down to the bend, turning left to the Villa I Tatti, once the home of world-famous art historian, Bernard Berenson (1865–1959) and now a Centre for Italian Renaissance Studies. The road continues to descend gently to Ponte a Mensola.

Fiesole's Roman theatre, still used during the summer arts festival

PONTE A MENSOLA

This hamlet stands in an idyllic spot with a little river running through it. Look for the two plaques which record the extraordinary number of famous English and American authors who were attracted to this region. Boccaccio spent his childhood here and used one of its buildings, the Villa di Poggio Gherardo, as the setting for some of the early scenes in the _Decameron_.
Turn left and continue on into Settignano.

SETTIGNANO

This delightful little town still maintains an independent life, despite being so close to Florence, and it is not as overwhelmed by tourists as Fiesole. Desiderio da Settignano (1430–64), the early Renaissance sculptor, grew up here and is commemorated by a statue.
From the main square the No 10 bus will take you back to Florence.

Arezzo

*A*rezzo is a large and bustling city with a population of around 90,000. Wartime bombing took its toll of the city, although happily the major monuments escaped, and there has been a considerable amount of modern building to the south. Nevertheless, recent development has been kept outside the city walls, and traffic has now been banned from the centre of what was, until quite recently, one of the most traffic-choked cities in Tuscany.

The copy of the startling *Chimera* statue stands near the railway station providing a clue to Arezzo's origins. The ancient Etruscan statue, discovered near the city in 1555, dates from the 5th century BC when Arezzo was one of the leaders of the Etruscan federation called the Dodecapolis (the Twelve Cities) which controlled central Tuscany before Rome flexed its muscles and took over all Italy. It remained an important city during the Romans and Maecenas, the wealthy patron of Horace and Virgil, was born here.

In the turbulent Middle Ages Arezzo was famous – or notorious – for its warrior bishops who ruled the city and led its citizens into many a battle in defence of their independence. In the end, like so many cities in Tuscany, it fell under the rule of Florence.

In Arezzo you can see one of the supreme works of the Renaissance, the frescos of Piero della Francesca. It was also the birthplace of two key figures, Petrarch and Vasari, and of the monk, Guido d'Arezzo, who invented modern musical notation sometime in the early 11th century.

Location: 80km southeast of Florence.
Getting there: regular trains from Florence.
Tourist information: Piazza Risorgimento (tel: 0575 23952).

CASA DI PETRARCA (PETRARCH'S HOUSE)

Francesco Petrarca, better known as Petrarch, was born in Arezzo in July 1304 to a Florentine family that had been expelled during one of several political purges that took place in that city (Dante had been sent into exile at the same time).

The house of his birth was originally built in the late 13th century but was almost completely destroyed by a

Monument to Petrarch, Arezzo-born poet and humanist

bombing raid in 1943 and then rebuilt in 1948. Today it is the seat of the scholarly Accademia Petrarca, dedicated to studying the life and times of the man who became renowned all over Europe as a scholar, poet and humanist. His great sonnet sequence, inspired by his unrequited love for a mysterious woman called Laura, was enormously influential on other writers, including Shakespeare. The library is used to display manuscripts and published editions of his works as well as innumerable biographies. You can also see interesting historical photographs of Arezzo, including some that show the effects of war-time bombing.

Via dell'Orto 28 (tel: 0575 24700). Open: 10am–noon and 3pm–5pm. Closed Saturday afternoon, Sunday and bank holidays. Admission free.

CASA DI VASARI
(VASARI'S HOUSE)

Giorgio Vasari (1511–74) is often pilloried by art historians because of his sycophantic attitude to the Medici. He was, however, a very good draughtsman, a more-than-adequate architect and a prolific artist, even if much of his work is serviceable rather than inspired. His main claim to fame, however, is the fact that he was the very first art historian and his book, *Lives of the Most Excellent Painters, Sculptors and Architects*, contains illuminating biographies of the great artists of the Renaissance.

On the walls and ceilings in his over-decorated home he personally painted portraits of the greatest artists of his age. He also painted his own self-portrait in the main room overlooking the street – but in a very modest manner; he shows himself with his back to the observer sitting at a window seat and looking

A room with a view; giving the house a thorough airing

through a window – the same window and window seat that you can see in the room today.

Via XX Settembre 55. Open: Monday to Saturday, 9am–7pm; Sunday, 9am–1pm. Admission free (ring bell if closed).

DUOMO (CATHEDRAL)

Arezzo stands on a hill which slopes steadily upwards before coming to an abrupt halt, with cliffs dropping to the plain below. The commanding position at the top of the hill – with the city falling away on one side and open country, with a view towards the mountains, on the other – would seem to be the natural site for a major building. Considering the great age of the city, therefore, it is curious that no major building appeared here until the cathedral was commenced in 1276. Even then, work went ahead only sporadically and it was not until 1510 that it was completed. Even the bell tower, although it looks medieval, is in fact a 19th-century addition and the façade itself was not completed until the early years of this century.

The interior, though austere, is impressive. The stained-glass windows, a relatively rare art form in Italy, make an immediate impression. These are outstanding in quality and are the work of the 16th-century master, the Frenchman, Guillaume de Marcillat (William of Marseilles) who also painted the first three vaults of the nave.

In the right-hand aisle is the tomb of Pope Gregory X (1205–1276). In the manner of the period the tomb is a reused Roman sarcophagus of the 4th century. Gregory died in Arezzo on his

Arezzo cathedral: Virgin and Child with Pope Gregory X and St Donato

way back from France after proclaiming a crusade.

On the left-hand side of the nave is the most important monument in the cathedral, both from an historical and from an artistic point of view – the tomb of Bishop Guido Tarlati. He was the most warlike of the fighting bishops of Arezzo and he ruled the city from 1312 until his death in 1327, having crushed all internal dissent and having lead the city successfully in wars against Florence and Siena. The tomb is carved with scenes from the bishop's life but these are set high up on the wall and difficult to see – in order to appreciate the details you will have to buy one of the postcards or guides on sale in the church. Next to the tomb is a beautiful and mysterious fresco by Piero della Francesca showing Mary Magdalene holding the glass perfume jar whose contents she used to wipe the feet of Christ.
Via Ricasoli. Open: daily, 7am–12.30pm and 3pm–6.30pm. Admission free.

MUSEO ARCHEOLOGICO
Arezzo's excellent Archaeological Museum occupies part of a 16th-century monastery built up against the curving side of the Roman amphitheatre; the windows of the museum look out on to the amphitheatre itself, one of the best preserved in Tuscany (now a public garden entered from Via F Crispi). The museum houses a collection of Etruscan and Roman remains found in and around Arezzo and has a series of rooms devoted to the famous Aretine wares that were made in Arezzo between 50BC and AD70, pottery notable for its lively decorative scenes in low relief.
Via Margaritone. Open: Tuesday to Saturday, 9am–2pm; Sunday, 9am–1pm. Closed Monday. Admission charge.

Arezzo's Piazza Grande, the site of a monthly antiques market

MUSEO DEL DUOMO

This small museum contains works of art removed from the cathedral. They include frescos by Arezzo's own artist, Spinello Aretino (Aretino is the name for citizens of Arezzo) and paintings by Giorgio Vasari.

Via San Domenico. Open: Monday to Saturday, 9am–noon. Closed Sunday. Admission free.

MUSEO STATALE D'ARTE MEDIOEVALE E MODERNA

Despite its rather grand title (The State Museum of Modern and Medieval Art), this museum is 'local' in the best sense of the word. It is housed in the handsome 15th-century Palazzo Bruni which modestly occupies the corner of two streets. The courtyard is worth looking at in its own right for it is probably the work of Bernardo Rossellino (1409–64). It is used to display a great variety of interesting sculptural fragments brought here from other buildings in the city. Most of the paintings on display within the museum are the work of local artists. Vasari, Arezzo's most successful self-publicist, has an immense work entitled *The Banquet of Esther and Ahasuerus*. Vasari used his wife as the model for Esther.

Via San Lorentino 8 (tel: 0575-300301). Open: Monday to Saturday, 9am–7pm; Sunday, 9am–1.30pm. Admission charge.

PIAZZA GRANDE

The Piazza Grande starts at the core of the historic city. A new centre of commercial life has now developed further down the hill so that this ancient square is now a charming and tranquil backwater. Most of the shops around the square specialise in antiques and it is here that a large and popular antiques market is held on the first Sunday of every month. It is also the setting for the Giostra del Saracino (Joust of the Saracen) festival, held every September (see page 148).

SAN FRANCESCO

Built in the early 14th century and never completed, this vast barn of a church contains one of the most compelling of all Renaissance fresco cycles, the *Legend of the True Cross* by Piero della Francesca (1416–92). This immense work occupies the whole of the sanctuary behind the high altar and it traces the history of the wood of the Cross from the tree planted by Adam down to the rediscovery of the buried Cross by St Helena, mother of the Emperor Constantine the Great.
Piazza San Francesco. Open: summer, Monday to Saturday, 8am–7pm; winter, Monday to Saturday, 8.30am–noon and 1.30pm–6.30pm; Sunday, no tourist visits. Admission free.

SANTA MARIA, PIEVE DI

The distinctive bell tower of Santa Maria is known as 'the tower of a hundred holes' because of its many openings. The façade, though weathered, is a splendid example of Romanesque decorative work. Inside, this grand Romanesque church, built at the turn of the 12th and 13th centuries, is solemn and austere. Most of the ornamentation is in the form of carving but there is a polyptych by Pietro Lorenzetti in the choir.
Corso Italia. Open: daily, 9am–1pm and 3pm–6pm. Admission free.

ETRUSCAN NEIGHBOURS

Chiusi and Cortona are both delightful little cities that will extend your knowledge of the ancient Etruscans. Both cities can be reached by train from Arezzo; the station for Cortona is at Camucia, 5km away, but with a regular bus service between the station and Cortona. There is also a regular bus service between Arezzo and Cortona.

CHIUSI

This ancient city was known to the Etruscans as *Camars* and its king was the famous Lars Porsena who lay siege to Rome in 510BC. Underneath the medieval city lies an immense necropolis and some of the ancient Etruscan tombs have wall paintings. Guided tours can be arranged at the Archaeological Museum which also contains a number of Etruscan artefacts, including carved sarcophagi.

PIERO DELLA FRANCESCA

Piero della Francesca (1420–92) is regarded as one of the great artists of the early Renaissance on the strength of just a handful of frescos. Of these, the *Story of the True Cross* can be seen in Arezzo but to see what art historians have called 'the greatest picture in the world' you must go to the little town of Sansepolcro, 39km northeast of Arezzo, on the Tuscan/Umbrian border. Here, in the Museo Civico (in the Palazzo Communale), visitors queue for a glimpse of della Francesca's *Resurrection* fresco. The picture, like all this artist's work, has a mysterious, dream-like quality quite unlike any other art of the time – Kenneth Clark, the art historian who wrote the definitive account of della Francesca's work, described it as expressing 'values for which no rational statement is adequate'. Equally awe-inspiring is the same artist's *Madonna del Parto* (Pregnant Madonna) fresco which can be seen in the tiny hilltop town of Monterchi, mid-way between Arezzo and Sansepolcro.

Museum open: Tuesday to Friday, 9am–1.45pm; Saturday and Sunday, 9am–1pm. Closed Monday. Admission charge.

CORTONA

This enchanting little hilltop town, which seems to float high above the Val di Chiana plain, is even older than Chiusi; legend claims that it was founded by Dardanus, who later founded Troy. Impossible to prove, this nevertheless ties in with the theory that the Etruscans came from Asia Minor. Situated at over 600m above sea level, the city is virtually one vast fortress with its steep, narrow streets and superb vistas.

The Museo dell'Accademia Etrusca occupies a 13th-century palace and contains medieval and Renaissance artefacts as well as many important Etruscan finds. The Museo Diocesana in the Piazza del Duomo contains works by Cortona's most important Renaissance

artist, Luca Signorelli (1441-1523) but the star of the collection is Fra Angelico's delicate *Annunciation* altarpiece.

The tourist office is in Via Nazionale (tel: 0575 630352).

Museo dell'Accademia Etrusca, Piazza Signorelli (tel: 0575 630415). Open: summer, 10am–1pm and 4pm–7pm; winter, 9am–1pm and 3pm–5pm. Closed Monday, April to September and winter. Admission charge.

Museo Diocesana, Piazza dell'Duomo. Open: summer, 9am–6.30pm; winter times vary between 9am–5pm. Closed Monday. Admission charge.

Right: Roman sarcophagus in Cortona's Museo Diocesana

Below: antiques and crafts for sale in Arezzo

Arezzo Town Walk

This walk will take you through the heart of the historic city. *Allow 1 hour.*

Begin at the railway station forecourt.

1 STAZIONE

The station marks the division between the historic city on its hill (population around 14,000) and the modern city on the plain outside the walls (population 80,000). Look for the Chimera Fountain on the right, on the other side of Via Spinello. This is an excellent copy of the ancient Etruscan

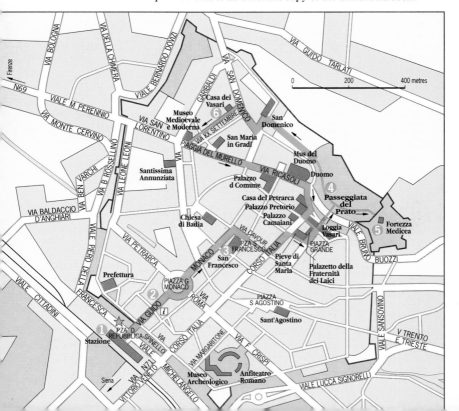

statue – depicting the mythological beast – part lion, part goat, part serpent – that was found near Arezzo in 1555 (the original can be seen in Florence – see page 48).

2 VIA GUIDO MONACO

Immediately opposite the station is the beginning of the modern Via Guido Monaco, a handsome avenue crowned at the top by the battlemented tower of the medieval Palazzo Municipale. The road is named after Guido d'Arezzo, a monk who, in about the year 1020, invented the system of musical notation on which all modern music is based. His statue stands in the pleasant little tree-shaded piazza, half way up the avenue. *Walk all the way up Via Guido Monaco and turn right at the top into Piazza San Francesco.*

3 SAN FRANCESCO

On the right is the immense church of San Francesco which contains one of the supreme works of the Italian Renaissance, the fresco of Piero della Francesca (see page 82). *Turn right out of the church and walk along Via Cavour, then turn left up Corso Italia; this is Arezzo's historic 'spinal cord' which links the city's lower and upper halves. Turn right past Pieve di Santa Maria with its striking campanile (see page 82). This will bring you into the Piazza Grande (page 82). Cross the piazza heading for the left-hand corner and ascend the flight of steps up to the Passegiata del Prato.*

4 PASSEGIATA DEL PRATO

The Passegiata, a public park, is popular with mothers with small children and, after school hours, with energetic young footballers. A green, quiet, tree-shaded spot, it is ideal for a restful hour or so and there is even a tiny open-air bar for refreshments.
Cross the Passegiata to the right to the Fortezza Medicea.

5 FORTEZZA MEDICEA

A long, grim tunnel will take you up to the centre of the fortress which has been landscaped to form an extension of the park. Follow the rampart round for a view of the modern city and of the still relatively unspoiled valley of the Casentino. Not far up that valley the Battle of Campaldino was fought betwen Florence and Arezzo in 1289. The poet Dante Alighieri took part in the battle and though Florence won, so many citizen-soldiers died on both sides that, thereafter, most Italian cities hired foreign mercenaries to fight on their behalf (see page 98).
Return to the Passeggiata and walk to the far side, to the east end of the Duomo (Cathedral). From the flight of steps there is an excellent view to the right of the city wall. The open space alongside the wall is now used as a market garden, showing how the population of the historic centre has shrunk. Turn left, then right into Via San Domenico, then left down Via XX Settembre.

6 CASA DEI VASARI

On the right of this street, part way down, is the Casa di Vasari, home of one of Arezzo's most famous citizens (see page 79).
The steeply descending street will take you down to the Piaggia del Murello. Turn left and climb up past the Duomo (see page 79) to return to the Piazza Grande. Here you can enjoy a much-deserved drink (or meal) at one of the open-air restaurants in the Loggia Vasari, located on the north side of the square and designed by Vasari in 1573.

Carrara

*T*his ancient city presents a dramatic example of the ability of Tuscan cities to maintain their identity over many centuries. Carrara is the marble capital of the world – the city's very name is derived from the ancient Etruscan word *kar* meaning 'stone'. The Romans came here for top-quality marble, as did Michelangelo and as do numerous modern architects and sculptors. Today, some half a million tonnes are exported annually and, as a consequence, Carrara has undergone an enormous expansion since World War II. The entire area between the old city and the resort of Marina di Carrara, on the coast 4km away, is now a solid mass of buildings.

Nevertheless, once you have driven up the seemingly endless Viale XX Settembre which bisects this sprawl, you will come into the old city. Towering around it are the sharp-pointed peaks of the Apuan Alps, whose summits look white, as if they were covered in snow, even in summer; in fact you are looking at the gleaming white marble of Carrara. Tumbling through the centre of the city is a milk-white mountain stream. All along its banks, and up into the mountains, small marble-processing workshops use water from the stream to wash away the dust and keep the cutting equipment cool.

Location: 126km north of Florence and 55km north of Pisa. Getting there: Carrara is on the main coastal railway line from Pisa. The station is at Carrara Avenza, 3km from the historic city centre. There are frequent bus connections (the bus terminal is on Piazza Matteotti). Tourist information: Piazza 2 Guilio (tel: 0585 843 370).

ACCADEMIA DI BELLE ARTI (SCHOOL OF FINE ARTS)

The Accademia is housed in one of the grim fortresses which stud this area of Tuscany. This one was turned into a palace in the 16th century and now forms a majestic backdrop to the Piazza Gramsci. The courtyard is open to the public and is used to display a number of ancient Roman sculptures.

Piazza Accademia.

DUOMO (CATHEDRAL)

Tucked away on the intimate little Piazza del Duomo, this is Carrara's principal monument. It is a child of the mountains for the marble from which it is built was quarried just up the road. The 11th-century building is in the same Romanesque style as the cathedrals of Pisa and Lucca, though on a smaller scale. The west front is particularly impressive, with its colonnades and a superb rose window, the latter inserted in the 14th century. The interior contains several sculptures in marble and wood of the 14th and 15th centuries. Outside, in the Piazza del Duomo, there is a 13th-century campanile and an unfinished statue by the Florentine, Baccio Bandinelli. Near by a plaque identifies the house where Michelangelo stayed when working in the quarries.

Piazza del Duomo. Open: daily, 8am–1pm and 3.30pm–6pm. Admission free. However, the Duomo has been closed for repairs for some time with no clear opening date. Check with Carrara Tourist Office.

CARRARA TOWN PLAN

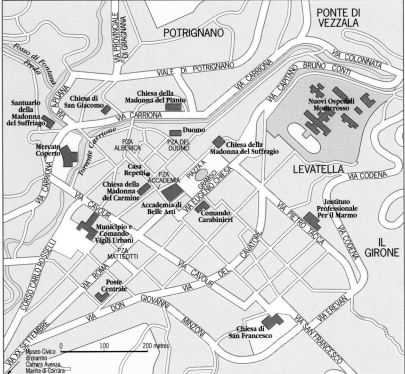

PONTE DI VEZZALA

POTRIGNANO

VIA PROVINCIALE DI GRAGNANA

VIALE DI POTRIGNANO

VIA COLONNATA

VIA CARRIONA

VIA CAPITANO BRUNO CONTI

Fosso di Fontana Preda

A. PUANA

Chiesa di San Giacomo

Chiesa della Madonna del Pianto

Santuario della Madonna del Suffragio

VIA CARRIONA

Duomo

Nuovi Ospedali Monterosso

Torrente Carrione

Mercato Coperto

PZA ALBERICA

PZA DEL DUOMO

Chiesa della Madonna del Suffragio

VIA CARRIONA

Casa Repetti

PZA ACCADEMIA

PIAZZA GRAMSCI

LEVATELLA

VIA CODENA

VIA CAVOUR

Chiesa della Madonna del Carmine

Accademia di Belle Arti

VIA EUGENIO CHIESA

Comando Carabinieri

Instituto Professionale Per il Marmo

VIA PIETRO TACCA

VIA CODENA

IL GIRONE

CORSO CARLO ROSSELLI

Municipio e Comando Vigili Urbani

PZA MATTEOTTI

DEL CAVALIERE

VIA ROMA

Poste Centrale

VIA CAVOUR

VIA DON GIOVANNI MINZONI

VIA EREVAN

VIA SAN FRANCESCO

VIA XX SETTEMBRE

Museo Civico di marmo Carrara Avenza, Marina di Carrara

Chiesa di San Francesco

0   100   200 metres

MUSEO CIVICO DI MARMO (CITY MARBLE MUSEUM)

The museum is located on the right-hand side of the Viale XX Settembre going down towards the coast and 2km from the city centre. Buses run there from Piazza Matteotti. The sculptures on display are of no great artistic merit but the museum tells a clear story of how marble is produced and used. *Viale XX Settembre. Open: May to September, Monday to Friday, 10am–1pm and 3.30pm–6.30pm. Admission charge.*

PIAZZA ALBERICA

This café-lined street is the social heart of Carrara. Although there is no building of outstanding importance, the 16th-century palaces which surround it collectively make up a superb townscape.

PIAZZA GRAMSCI

This is the only green open space in the old city centre. The square's main feature is a quite extraordinary fountain consisting of a large marble sphere being turned round by tiny jets of water.

QUARRIES

The Emperor Augustus boasted that he found Rome built in brick, and left it in marble. All over Italy other cities followed suit, cladding their important buildings in the same beautiful, polished, gleaming stone. Much of that marble came from Carrara; sculptors in particular used the flawless stone for their major works. The quarries fell into decline in the early Middle Ages but received a tremendous boost during the Renaissance. Michelangelo was a familiar figure here in the 16th century, spending days clambering around the quarries looking for the perfect

stone for his work. In one of his letters he recounts the difficulties involved in moving the huge blocks of marble intended for St Peter's. He also made the point that the Florentine stone-workers he brought with him were of little use, being unskilled in the handling of marble. Even today, the Carrarese marble-workers have a skill that few can equal.

Despite the millions of tonnes of marble that have been extracted from the hills around Carrara, millions more remain. Quarrying began in Roman times and still goes on, making this one of the world's oldest industrial sites in continuous use. The Romans extracted the marble by hammering pegs of figwood into natural fissures, then pouring water over them so that they expanded and cracked the stone. In the

Images of Carrara's
marble quarrying
industry

19th century gunpowder was used, with harmful effects on the stone – as shown by the deterioration of the façade of Florence cathedral. Today the stone is cut with a continuous wire band saw, hundreds of metres in length, which moves slowly forward on pulleys. A typical Carrara quarry presents an unforgettable sight: blindingly white against the blue sky, the blocks and steps of marble look like titanic buildings or sculptures.

To visit one of the quarries of Carrara, take the old road signposted to Colonnata that leads eastward from Carrara city centre into the mountains. Once you reach Colonnata, 8km from the city centre, you will see plenty of signs saying *Cave di Marmo*, indicating a quarry.

Lucca

*E*ven in a country where the preservation of historic city centres is regarded as the norm, rather than a cause to be fought for, Lucca stands out. It is a large city, with a population of around 93,000 (in the same league as Pisa) but most of them live in the suburbs. This leaves the historic centre, shielded by its enormous walls, an unspoiled gem of a Tuscan city.

Lucca is Roman in origin (Caesar, Pompey and Crassus met here to form the First Triumvirate) and one of the city's most intriguing sights is the Roman amphitheatre (see below). The city also has an unusually high number of good medieval and Renaissance palaces and more than its fair share of impressive Romanesque churches.

The resplendent former bishop of Lucca who later became Pope Alexander II

Unlike other characterful Tuscan cities, such as Montepulciano, Lucca is by no means off the beaten track. On the contrary, its near neighbours are the booming industrial cities of Pisa and Pistoia. A major international airport lies almost at its doorstep and it is on a main railway line. The city is therefore fully in touch with the 20th century. Its citizens are among the most prosperous in Italy, drawing their wealth partly from the soil (the province of Lucca produces some of

Italy's best olive oil) and from small family firms in the city itself.

Lucca, however, has learned to take the best of the 20th century while controlling the rest. Long before many other European cities realised the destructive effects of heavy traffic, the Lucchese set about barring it from the area within the city walls. Some could argue that this was far less of a hardship than it might have been, because Lucca is totally flat and quite unlike the steep, hilly towns of central Tuscany. The Lucchese have thus adopted cycling as their preferred form of transport and within the city walls the bicycle is used by young and old alike (visitors can hire bicycles at the tourist office in Piazzale G Verdi).

Location: 74km west of Florence, 22km northeast of Pisa. Getting there: Lucca is on the main railway line connecting Viareggio to Florence via Pisa and there is a regular bus service from both Florence and Pisa. Tourist information: Piazza Guidiccioni 2 (tel: 0583 41205).

ANFITEATRO

Lucca's main street is the Via Fillungo and this lives up to its name (which means 'long thread') by being little more than a narrow lane winding its way between high buildings. Just off its northern section is the Roman amphitheatre (also known as the Piazza Mercato). There are many Roman

Above: the birthplace of Puccini, composer of
Tosca and *Madame Butterfly*
Right: Casa Guinigi roof garden

amphitheatres in Italy but none so odd
as this. The amphitheatre itself has gone
but its shape is perfectly preserved like a
fossil by the houses that were built up
against its outer wall. These houses now
form an elliptical circuit and the four
entrances into the piazza occupy the
same position as the original four gates
into the amphitheatre.

CASA GUINIGI

It is not difficult to track down this
massive town house of the Guinigi
family because there is an oak tree
growing from the top of its great tower.
Built in red brick in the 14th century,
the palace was the home of Lucca's
ruling family. The great tower is open to

the public and the remarkable little
garden on the top, as well as the
breathtaking views over the city, make it
well worth a visit.
*Via Sant'Andrea. Tower open: summer,
daily, 9am–7pm; winter, daily,
10am–4pm. Admission charge.*

CASA DI PUCCINI

The birthplace of Giacomo Puccini
(1858–1924) has been set out as a
shrine to one of Italy's most popular
operatic composers. Quite apart from its
association with Puccini, the building is
of interest in itself as a good example of
a 15th-century town house. The objects
on display range from the Steinway
grand piano on which Puccini composed
Turandot down to his hat and overcoat.
Evidence of the national adulation he
enjoyed is provided by the remarkable
series of postcards which feature his

haughty face – looking more like a
business tycoon than a composer. There
are also holograph letters and original
designs for the costumes used in his
operas.
*Corte San Lorenzo 9. Open: summer,
10am–6pm; winter, 10am–4pm. Closed
Monday all year. Admission charge.*

DUOMO (CATHEDRAL)

It is well worth pausing to look at the façade of the cathedral of San Martino before entering. Not only does this contain some of the most interesting details of the building, it also represents the last echo of the Romanesque style which influenced churches all over Europe in the 10th to 13th centuries and which characterises so many of Lucca's fine churches. The cathedral was founded in the 6th century and rebuilt between 1060 and 1070, although the façade was not added until 1204. The inlaid marble work on the façade is a *tour de force* and an excellent example of the so-called Pisan Romanesque style. Among the best details are the bas reliefs showing the *Nativity* and the *Deposition*, attributed to Nicola Pisano (by the left-hand door). There is also a fascinating *Tree of Life*, with Adam and Eve at the bottom, and a series of panels depicting the Labours of the Months (a popular medieval subject) which provide a lively picture of everyday rural life in the 13th century.

The interior was largely rebuilt between 1370 to 1490 and is rather gloomy. The dominant feature is the marble Tempietto or tabernacle (1484) by Matteo Civitali, Lucca's most important native artist. The Tempietto shelters one of Europe's most potent relics, the so-called Volto Santo or 'Holy Face'. The figure on the crucifix is said to be a true portrait of Christ, carved by Nicodemus who witnessed the Crucifixion and helped take Christ's body down from the Cross. Legend has it that the crucifix came to Lucca by supernatural means and throughout the Middle Ages it was a major object of European pilgrimage (and hence a considerable source of revenue to the cathedral authorities). Scholars now believe it was carved in the 12th or 13th century but this fact does not deter the faithful who take part in a torchlight procession through the city, preceded by the holy image, every year on 13 September.

The low lighting makes it difficult to appreciate the remainder of the cathedral's interior details. On the third altar on the right is Tintoretto's *Last Supper*. The Sacristy has a *Maesta* (Virgin Enthroned) by Ghirlandaio and there is another, by Fra Bartolomeo, in the Sanctuary. The most beautiful object, however, is the glimmering white marble tomb, in the left-hand aisle, of Ilaria del Carretto (1406), carved by the Sienese artist, Jacopo della Quercia. Ilaria, who died young, was the wife of Paolo Guinigi of the all-powerful clan that ruled Lucca. Della Quercia has shown her as an exquisitely graceful young woman asleep with her little dog at her feet.

Piazza del Duomo. Open: daily, 9am–noon and 3.30pm–5.30pm. Admission free.

MUSEO DELL'OPERA DEL DUOMO (CATHEDRAL WORKS MUSEUM)

This new museum shows how ultra-modern display techniques can be used to good effect in a medieval building. The museum houses the jewels which are used to decorate the Volto Santo on ceremonial occasions and other objects are in the process of being transferred here from the cathedral (it is possible that the Ilaria del Carreto tomb will be among them).

Piazza Antelminelli 5 (tel: 0583-490530). Open: Tuesday to Sunday, 10am–1pm and 3pm–6pm. Closed Monday. Admission free.

MUSEO NAZIONALE

This museum is housed in the Villa Guinigi, another of the ruling family's town houses – this time an immense but plain Renaissance building in red brick tucked away on the eastern side of the town. The collection covers a wide range of displays, from archaeological finds to domestic furniture. There is a particularly interesting group of Romanesque reliefs. The picture gallery contains works by Lucchese and Sienese artists.

Via della Quarquonia. Open: Tuesday to Sunday, 9am–2pm. Closed Monday. Admission charge.

ORTO BOTANICO (BOTANICAL GARDEN)

Founded in 1820, this delightful garden is of great botanical interest and provides one of the few green areas within the city walls.

The entrance to the garden is on the city wall from Baluardo San Regolo (tel: 0583-46665). Open: daily, 9am–noon. Admission charge.

PALAZZO PFANNER

This museum is in the process of restoration but should be well worth a visit when it reopens. It houses a major collection of 17th- and 18th-century costume, including fine examples of the silk garments which made Lucca wealthy. The 18th-century garden (visible from the city walls) is small but delightfully laid out with statuary.

Via Battisti.

PIAZZA NAPOLEONE

The dizzying political upheavals of the early 19th century turned Lucca into a dukedom for the Bourbons in 1817. This sprawling, graceless square, largely used as a daytime car park, was their gift to the city. The immense building on

The fine formal garden to the rear of the Palazzo Pfanner

The façade of San Michele

section of the façade soars up into thin air. The figure of St Michael, flanked by trumpet-blowing angels, crowns the façade and the angels really do look as though they are about to fly off.

PINACOTECA NAZIONALE
The main interest of this picture gallery is the building itself, the 17th-century Palazzo Mansi. Much of the original palace furnishings have survived and the focal point of interest is undoubtedly the bridal chamber and antechamber, a masterpiece of unrestrained vulgarity in gold and crimson velvet. The paintings, with portraits predominating, are displayed much as they would have been when this was still in use as a family mansion. Among them are a number of gross Medici cardinals and Bronzino's portrait of Cosimo I which fully brings out his ruthless nature.
Via Galli Tassi (tel: 0583-55570). Open: Tuesday to Saturday, 9am–7pm; Sunday, 9am–2pm. Closed Monday. Admission charge.

SAN FREDIANO
This is another of Lucca's fine and unspoiled Romanesque churches, built between 1112 and 1147 and virtually unaltered since. The façade is enlivened by a superb 13th-century mosaic of *The Ascension,* best seen after dark when the floodlighting creates a blaze of gold. The great font inside dates from the same period as the church, its carvings by at least three different artists, all anonymous but all of the first rank. In the chapel behind the font is displayed the 'uncorrupted' body of St Zita, a pathetic mummy dressed up in incongruous finery which is brought out on the saint's feast day (26 April) for the citizens to touch. Zita was a servant girl

the western side of the square was originally the seat of the republican council but because it was occupied by the Bourbons it has been known as the Palazzo Ducale ever since. Despite its lack of architectural charm, the piazza is one of the liveliest places in Lucca. Immediately adjoining it is the Piazza del Giglio, site of Lucca's highly popular theatre, the Teatro Giglio.

PIAZZA SAN MICHELE
This piazza stands on the site of the Roman forum and it is still a popular meeting place for Lucca's citizens, testimony to the inate conservatism of Italian cities. In the loggia on the south side is a modern statue of Lucca's only major artist, Matteo Civitali (1435–1501). He began life as a barber but finished as a sculptor and architect. Dominating the piazza is the church of San Michele with its truly amazing façade. This was built first and then the money ran out before the nave could be completed – that is why the upper

Above: the baroque Villa Mansi, north of Lucca
Left: San Frediano with its 13th-century
Ascension mosaic

who was admonished by her master for
giving food to the poor. She is also the
patron saint of servants. In the
neighbouring chapel are 16th-century
frescos depicting, among other subjects,
the bringing of the Volto Santo to Lucca
and San Frediano saving Lucca from a
flood.
*Piazza San Frediano. Open: daily,
8am–1pm and 4pm–6pm. Admission free.*

SANTA MARIA FORISPORTAM

The main interest of this church lies in
its name and its façade. Forisportam
('outside the gates') indicates that the
church was built outside the first circuit
of the Roman walls and gives some
indication as to how the city has grown,
for Santa Maria is now well within the
main circuit. The façade is 13th-century
Pisan Romanesque, unusually plain for
that style but harmonious.
Via Santa Croce.

Lucca Town Walls

This walk takes you along the top of Lucca's well-preserved 16th-century city walls. Lucca's walls are so immense that they have a road along the top, some 4km long, shaded by an avenue of trees. Walking the entire circuit is the best way to get a general view of the city and an added attraction – especially for children – is that you can hire bicycles to ride along the walls. *Allow 1 hour.*

Lucca's walls were begun in 1500 and took over 150 years to build. They were specifically designed to withstand an artillery attack and they are immensely thick, measuring 30m wide at the base. The walls were further surrounded by a complex system of earthworks and ditches, originally intended as part of the defences and now maintained as an attractive green park which serves to separate the historic city centre from the

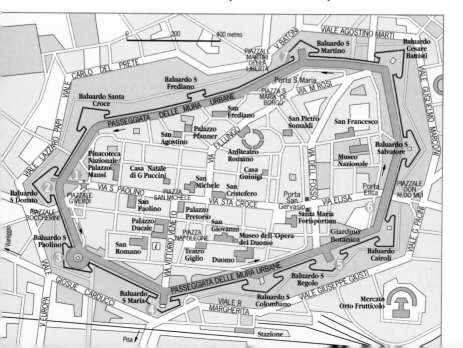

chaotic ring road that runs around Lucca. At regular intervals round the walls there are 11 immense spade-shaped *baluardi* (bastions) and six gates. Ironically, the walls were never attacked and so have survived in near-perfect condition. Marie Louise de Bourbon, the governor of the city in the early 19th century, had the top of the walls planted with a magnificent double row of plane, lime, oak and chestnut trees.
Start at the Piazzale G Verdi.

1 PIAZZALE G VERDI
You can hire bicycles at the tourist office in this piazza. The tourist office occupies one of the old city gates which was superseded when the present circuit of walls was built outside the medieval circuit.
Go up the ramp of the Baluardo San Donato, which stands to the right of the city gate, and then turn left to follow the Passegiata delle Mura Urbane, the road that runs along the top of the walls.

2 BALUARDO SAN DONATO
The isolated building on the left is the headquarters of the Company of Lucchese Crossbowmen. Founded in 1443, the Company is still active and puts on a splendid show at the feast of San Paolino, the city's patron saint, in July. The plaque on the wall commemorates Castruccio Castracani who, in the early 14th century, freed Lucca from the control of Pisa and conquered a number of smaller surrounding cities. The Company put up the plaque to him in 1981, the 700th anniversary of his birth.

3 BALUARDO SAN PAOLINO
The next bastion along houses the headquarters of the International Institute for the Study of City Walls (CISCU). The bastion's interior is honeycombed with chambers and passages which were once used as barracks for the city garrison and stables for the horses. Tours can be arranged (tel: 0583 46257).

4 BALUARDO SANTA MARIA
The next bastion has been laid out as a delightful garden, with a café and restaurant. As you continue you will see the tall cathedral campanile on the left. From the next bastion, Baluardo San Colombano, you will get a good view of the cathedral itself.

5 BALUARDO SAN REGOLO
Here is the entry to the Orto Botanico (Botanical Garden). You can get a good view of the garden from a little further along the wall.

6 PORT ELISA
Just beyond the next bastion, Baluardo Cairoli, is one of the city gates, Port Elisa. If you look left along the road which runs into the city from this gate you will see another massive gate, the Porta San Gervasio, part of the older city wall.
Continue on past Baluardo San Salvatore and Baluardo Cesare Battisti to Baluardo San Martino.

7 BALUARDO SAN MARTINO
This protects one of the city's six gates, the Porta Santa Maria which leads out on to a bustling piazza. A little further along, beyond the next bastion, the Baluardo San Frediano, there is an excellent view into the formal 18th-century garden of Palazzo Pfanner. Pass one more bastion, Santa Croce, and you will be back at the start.

MERCENARIES

At the battle of Campaldino, fought in 1289 between Arezzo and Florence, the slaughter of citizen-soldiers on both sides was so great that it gave even the battled hardened city-states pause for thought. Gradually, mercenaries from that time on began to take over the fighting. These mercenaries were often foreign (a foreign soldier was regarded as having no interest in local politics) with English, Germans and Hungarians predominating. They formed themselves into companies of about

Piero Uccello's *The Battle of San Romano*

5,000 men under the command of a *condottiero*, so called because he would negotiate a *condotta* (a form of contract) with a particular city; this stipulated that his company would serve the city for a set period of time for a set sum. When that period was finished, the *condottiero* was free to find another employer – even if (as was

often the case) this was the enemy of their previous employer.

The main aim of every mercenary was to avoid being killed whilst making a lot of money. City-state warfare thus became a little like modern wrestling – it was not unknown for the mercenaries to fake the battle, having decided among themselves, in advance, who was going to emerge the winner.

One *condottiero* who did not play to these rules was the feared Englishman, John Hawkwood, whom the Tuscans nicknamed Giovanni Acuto (literally John Sharp). Born in Essex in about 1320, he fought in France under the Black Prince. During one of the truces of the Hundred Years War he travelled to Italy and formed the White Company, composed of 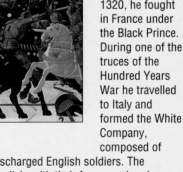 discharged English soldiers. The English, with their fearsome longbows and superb discipline, rapidly came to dominate the battlefields.

Hawkwood was a rarity among *condottieri* in that he could not be bribed and always honoured his contract exactly. In 1377 the Florentines made him their Captain General, in supreme

Sir John Hawkwood in Uccello's memorial fresco

command of all military forces in the city and even, on occasions, charged with policing the turbulent citizens. The city council promised him a handsome equestrian statue after his death. When the time came, however, they thriftily decided to settle for a wall painting instead. They did, though, commission Paolo Uccello to paint this commemorative fresco, which can be seen in the cathedral (see page 47). Uccello used the new *chiaroscuro* technique which at least gave the fresco the appearance of a three-dimensional stone monument.

Montepulciano

*A*part from the peace, and its famous Vino Nobile, Montepulciano's chief attraction is architectural, for it is a perfect miniature Renaissance city with a remarkable number of outstanding palaces. Many are the work of the Florentine architect, Antonio Sangallo the Elder (1455–1537), who came to Montepulciano in 1511.

Traffic has been almost totally banned from Montepulciano and the best way to explore the city is simply to follow the Corso, the wide main road which winds up from Porta al Prato gate at the lower end of the town all the way round to the Piazza Grande on the crest of the hill, upon which the major public buildings are to be found.

Location: 119km southeast of Florence, 36km southeast of Siena. Getting there: Montepulciano is about 1½ hours by bus from Siena. The nearest railway station is Chiusi-Chianciano, on the Siena to Rome line. Buses connect this station to Montepulciano. Tourist information: Piazza Don Minzoni (tel: 0578 757442). Open: Tuesday to Sunday, 10am–noon and 4pm–6pm.

MONTEPULCIANO

DUOMO (CATHEDRAL)

The elegant late Renaissance cathedral has one outstanding work of art: the *Assumption of the Virgin* altarpiece by Taddeo di Bartolo (1401).
Piazza Grande. Open: daily, 7am–12.15pm and 4pm–7pm. Admission free.

MUSEO CIVICO

The most interesting feature of this museum is probably the building itself. This is one of Montepulciano's many fine palaces, the Palazzo Neri-Orselli, and it was built in the Sienese Gothic style. The collection includes some terracottas from the della Robbia workshops and a number of paintings, mostly 16th-century, by local artists.
Via Ricci 10. Open: summer, Wednesday to Sunday, 9.30am–1pm and 3pm–6pm (closed Monday and Tuesday); winter, by request only to Biblioteca Comunale, Via Ricci 10 (tel: 0578-716935). Admission charge.

The hill town of Montepulciano rises high above San Biagio church

PALAZZO COMUNALE

Montepulciano's little 14th-century Palazzo Comunale is a flattering copy of the Palazzo Vecchio in Florence. It achieved this appearance when the façade was remodelled in the 15th century by the Florentine architect, Michelozzo. The tower is the main attraction and the ascent, via a number of ladders, is an interesting experience in its own right; from the top there is a superb view of the town and the surrounding countryside.

Piazza Grande. Open: Monday to Saturday, 8.30am–1.30pm. Closed Sunday. Admission free.

PIAZZA GRANDE

Laid out like a stage set on the highest point of the hill on which Montepulciano sits, this is the city's main square and it is surrounded by major public buildings. Look out for the splendid lion and griffin fountain in the northeast corner of the square, in front of the arcaded Palazzo Tarugi.

PORTA AL PRATO

Montepulciano was a prize over which both Florence and Siena fought. As soon as Florence gained control, Antonio

Sangallo was sent to strengthen its defences and this great gate, which is still the main entrance to the town, was his first work. Just beyond the gate is the Florentine symbol, the *marzocco*, a heraldic lion, raised on a pedestal (the original is in the Museo Civico).

SAN BIAGIO

You will have to leave the town to visit this church for it stands just outside the city walls to the southwest and is approached along a solemn avenue of cypresses. It is well worth the walk (allow about half an hour) for not only is this Antonio Sangallo's masterpiece, it is also set in the most beautiful rural surroundings.

Off the N146 Pienza road. Open: daily, 9am–1.30pm and 3pm–5pm. Admission free.

TORRE DI PULCINELLA

This is one of Montepulciano's few surviving tower houses, dating back to the turbulent medieval period. On the roof is the extraordinary white figure of Pulcinella the clown, one of the characters from the *Commedia dell'Arte*, which strikes the hours on the town bell.

Piazza Michelozzo.

Pisa

*T*here is far more to Pisa than the famous Leaning Tower, yet the city suffers from a low profile. Visitors tend to arrive at the airport and spend perhaps a couple of hours in and around the Campo dei Miracoli before whisking off by train or coach to Florence or Siena.

In part this is because Pisa is overshadowed by Florence, barely an hour distant by train. But nature has also conspired against it. Whereas, in Florence, the Arno is still a living river crossed by four elegant and historic bridges, the Arno in Pisa is a sullen brown flood bordered by low-rise buildings and crossed by a series of nondescript modern bridges.

History

No one knows the precise origins of Pisa. Bronze Age artefacts have been discovered near the city and there are claims that Pisa was founded by the ancient Greeks. Roman remains, among

The Arno embankments in Pisa

them the ruins of the so-called Bagno di Nerone) Baths of Nero in Largo del Parlascio, show that this was an important imperial city.

But Pisa's great period began in the 11th century when, in a series of tremendous sea battles against Arabic ships, she won control of the western Mediterranean. In 1069, by defeating the Saracens of Sicily, the city won so colossal a booty as to pay for the superb

buildings on the Campo dei Miracoli, which launched an entirely new form of architecture. For the next 300 years or so, Pisa remained one of the great maritime cities of the Mediterranean. But, drawn into endless battles with neighbouring cities, Pisa eventually fell to Florence in 1406.

Pisa ceased to be a major port in the 16th century when Livorno became the main harbour in Tuscany. Since then the city has declined and, in the 19th century, the poet Shelley described it as 'a desolation of a city, which was the cradle and is now the grave of a distinguished people'.

In the closing months of World War II, the city was at the front line of the fighting between the advancing Allies and the retreating Germans, who faced each other on either side of the Arno; Allied bombers attacked the city on 31 August 1943, which suffered terribly as a consequence. Today Pisa has been rebuilt and is an important industrial and university city, one of the largest in Tuscany, with a population of over 100,000.

Orientation

The historic city centre is concentrated on the north bank of the river and is still surrounded by 12th-century walls. The 'high street' is the long and curving Via Santa Maria, which connects the Campo dei Miracoli with the Lungarno (Embankment). The palaces and mansion that line this street still retain their handsome façades dating from the 16th to the 18th centuries. Number 25 (built in 1595) has the bust of Duke Ferdinand I while the building at the end of the street is the Palazzo Reale, the royal palace of the Grand Dukes. Number 26 is the Domus Galileiana, named after Galileo, an 18th-century

building which once housed the Observatory and is now a scientific research centre.

The social centre of Pisa is the Piazza Garibaldi on the north side of the Ponte di Mezzo (Middle Bridge) and the elegant colonnaded Borgo Stretto which leads away from it.

Location: Pisa is 91km west of Florence. Getting there: Pisa Centrale station is on the main railway line between Galileo Galilei airport (Pisa Aeroporto station) and Florence. Tourist information: Piazza Arcivescovado 8 (tel: 050 560 464).

PISA TOWN PLAN

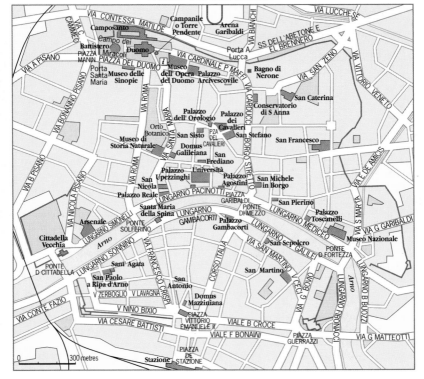

The Baptistery, like a papal crown

BATTISTERO (BAPTISTERY)

Begun in 1152 by Diotisalvi, the main body of the Baptistery was not completed until 1284 after Nicola Pisano and his son, Giovanni, added the splendid Gothic arcades of the upper storey. Even then, the Baptistery did not take its final form until the Gothic dome was added in the 14th century. The Pisani also carved the figures in the entrance portals (most of these are copies; the originals are now in the Museo dell'Opera del Duomo – see page 107). The circular shape of the Baptistery was inspired by the church of the Holy Sepulchre in Jerusalem and, because only a segment is visible at a time from outside, on stepping inside you receive the extraordinary impression that the immense interior is bigger than the exterior. The Baptistery is famous for its acoustics and is virtually empty of

furnishings except for the font by Guido da Como (1246) and Nicola Pisano's superb pulpit (1260). It is worth ascending the ramp within the Baptistery walls to reach the upper gallery to get a bird's-eye view of the building, and the unusual view of the Duomo façade.

Campo dei Miracoli (tel: 050 560 547). Open: summer, 9am–7pm; winter, 9am–6pm. Admission charge.

CAMPANILE (THE LEANING TOWER)

Work began on Pisa's famous Leaning Tower in 1173. By the time the tower had reached about a third of its intended height it began to lean because of the sandy and unstable nature of the subsoil. In attempting to correct this fault, successive architects built back at an angle so that the profile of the Tower is, in fact, a shallow crescent. The tower was completed in 1350, since when it has continued to tilt; the angle at which it is leaning is now 4.5m from the perpendicular, and steadily increasing. Experts predict that the tower will eventually collapse, and for at least the last 100 years architects of all nations have put forward various suggestions for checking the incline. Despite this, no foolproof solution has yet been found and since January 1990 the tower has been closed to the public while engineers rather desperately continue to seek a solution.

Campo dei Miracoli.

CAMPO DEI MIRACOLI (THE FIELD OF MIRACLES)

This is Pisa's great set piece, an immensè green lawn on which stand four great buildings in gleaming white marble – the Duomo (Cathedral), the

Battistero (Baptistery), the Campanile (Leaning Tower) and the Camposanto cemetery. Surrounding the Campo on two sides is the city wall. There are also two major museums on the south side: the Museo delle Sinopie contains the original sketches in plaster from the fire-damaged frescos of the Camposanto (open: summer, 9am–7pm; winter, 9am–6pm), and the Museo dell'Opera del Duomo (see page 107).

CAMPOSANTO

Camposanto literally means 'Holy Field' and this site was chosen as the city's main cemetery in the 13th century. It consists essentially of a rectangular cloister, built between the late 13th and early 15th centuries, surrounding a simple garden.

According to legend, earth for the cemetery was brought back from the Holy Land in the 13th century to be used for the burials of important people. Pisan notables, mostly clerical, are still buried here and the cloister has an outstanding range of funerary monuments, from ancient Roman sarcophagi to modern sculptures. Its walls were once covered with a series of 14th- and 15th-century frescos. An Allied incendiary bomb landed on the cemetery on the night of 27 July 1944 and destroyed most of these frescos. Those that survived include a substantial part of *The Triumph of Death* fresco, painted by an unknown master and commemorating the Black Death of 1348. For protection this, along with a spirited *Last Judgement* fresco, has been removed and placed under cover in one of the chambers off the north side of the cloister. There is also a display here of black and white photographs showing the frescos before the destruction.

Campo dei Miracoli (tel: 050 560 547). Open: summer, 9am–1pm and 3pm–8pm; winter, 9am–5pm. Admission charge.

Famously leaning, Pisa's Romanesque campanile, begun in 1173

DUOMO (CATHEDRAL)

Begun in 1063, Pisa's cathedral brings together three distinct architectural traditions – Roman, Islamic and Byzantine – fused together to create a unique new style, Pisan Romanesque. The 12th-century bronze doors of the Portale di San Ranieri (opposite the Leaning Tower) are the work of Bonanno da Pisa (the original architect of the tower); these too demonstrate

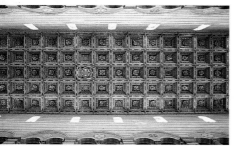

Eastern and western architectural styles meet in Pisa's cathedral

Pisan acquaintance with the Eastern Mediterranean, in the palm trees and other realistic details in the background to the Biblical scenes. The handsome façade facing the Baptistery, with its ascending tiers of colonnades, dates from the 13th century.

A disastrous fire in 1595 destroyed most of the works of art inside the cathedral. Among the survivors is the monumental pulpit by Giovanni Pisano (1302–10). It was removed after the fire and subsequently forgotten – it was not rediscovered and replaced until 1926 (to study its rich details be sure to have a good supply of L200 coins to activate the lights). Other survivals include the great mosaic of *Christ Enthroned*, by Cimabue (1302), in the apse and the noble tomb of the Holy Roman Emperor, Henry VII, who died in Pisa in 1313.

Campo dei Miracoli (tel: 050 560 547). Open: daily, 7.45am–12.45pm and 3pm–7pm (5pm winter). Admission charge.

LUNGARNI (EMBANKMENTS)

The embankments running alongside the Arno are lined with 16th-century palaces. Many are rich in history and deserve a closer look. Near the Ponte della Cittadella on the north bank is the Arsenal of the Medici. Behind the 18th-century façade at Lungarno Pacinotti 44 is a medieval tower house, while the façade of number 26 is a remarkable terracotta confection of the late 13th century. Just to the north of this embankment is the Palazzo Sapienza, the principal offices of Pisa's university, originally built in the 14th century and expanded by the Medici. At Lungarno Mediceo 30 (beyond Piazza Garibaldi) is the largely 16th-century Palazzo Toscanelli which Byron rented in 1821.

On the south bank, near the Ponte Solferino, standing in isolated splendour, is the exquisite little church of Santa Maria della Spina. Named after a thorn from Christ's crown, this was built in the 1320s.

MUSEO DELL'OPERA DEL DUOMO (CATHEDRAL WORKS MUSEUM)

This excellent modern museum occupies the original chapter house of the cathedral. There are intimate views of the Leaning Tower from the cloister. The museum contains numerous works of art including fine sculptures by the Pisani dating from the foundation of the cathedral down to the 19th century. On the upper floor is a brilliant display of coloured 19th-century engravings of the frescos in the Camposanto, showing just what has been lost.

Piazza Arcivescovado, near the Leaning Tower (tel: 050 560 547). Open: summer, 9am–7pm; winter, 9am–1pm and 3pm–5pm. Admission charge.

GALILEO GALILEI (1564–1642)

Galileo, the great mathematician and astronomer, the father of empirical science, was born in Pisa and it is said that his observation of the great lamp swinging in the cathedral gave him the idea of the pendulum. He also tested his theory of the speed of falling objects by dropping them from the Leaning Tower. The Inquisition condemned him for heresy in teaching that the earth went round the sun and not vice versa, and he was denied a Christian burial until 1737. In 1992 the Vatican finally conceded that his theory was correct.

Away from the tourist-besieged sights, Pisa is a good place to shop

ORTO BOTANICO (BOTANICAL GARDEN)

This delightful green spot in the heart of the city is one of the oldest botanical gardens in Europe; founded in the 1540s, it is now part of Pisa university.

Via L Ghini, just off Via S Maria (tel: 050 561 795). Open: Monday to Friday, 8am–1pm and 2pm–5.30pm; Saturday, 8am–1pm. Closed Sunday. Admission free.

PIAZZA DEI CAVALIERI

The original central square of medieval Pisa, the Piazza dei Cavalier was also probably the site of the Roman forum. Vasari redesigned the square for Duke Cosimo I whose statue stands in front of the strangely decorated Palazzo dei Cavalieri. To the left of this building is the Palazzo dell'Orologio, built in 1607 and incorporating the remains of a medieval tower. Dante tells the grim story of how Count Ugolino della Gherardesca, along with his sons and grandsons, was starved to death in 1288 by being walled up in this tower, having been tried and found guilty on false charges of treason.

San Gimignano

*A*s you approach San Gimignano, the distant view of this little town, with its soaring slender towers, looks just like an illumination in a medieval manuscript. San Gimignano is commonly referred to as the 'city of the beautiful towers' but these stern structures were not built for aesthetic reasons.

All Tuscan towns once had such towers, which are evidence of the violent conditions of life in medieval Italy. Each belonged to a family or a corporation, desperately striving to rise above their neighbours so that they could better defend themselves during times of riot by dropping missiles or burning pitch or oil on the enemy. Incredibly, there were once over 70 towers in this tiny hilltop town (compared with 100 in Florence) of which 13 survive.

San Gimignano has reversed the normal Tuscan trend, for its present population of around 7,500 is half what it was in the 16th century. It is small enough to be explored in a day (there is virtually no traffic) but it also makes a good base for country walks.

Location: 55km southwest of Florence, 38km northwest of Siena. Getting there: there are regular bus services from Florence and Siena, and scores of tour operators in both cities run daily excursions to San Gimignano. Tourist information: Piazza del Duomo 1 (tel: 0577 940 008).

SAN GIMIGNANO

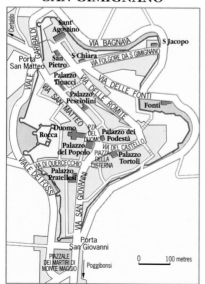

COLLEGIATA

San Gimignano's collegiate church is often called the Duomo (Cathedral) even though the town no longer has a bishop. The plain brick exterior of the 12th-century church gives no hint of the richness of its interior, modelled on Siena's cathedral. The entire expanse of the great nave walls is covered with a tremendous series of murals. The best time to see them is early in the morning, for there is little by way of natural light and the automatic lighting gulps up coins. The northern wall, painted in the 1360s by Bartolo di Fredi, illustrates events from the Old Testament in a delightfully naïve manner. The southern wall illustrates the Life of Christ. Also in this aisle is the Santa Fina chapel with charming frescos on the life of this girl saint by the Florentine artist, Ghirlandaio. On the west wall, high above the entrance, is a particularly

Chianti wines and wild boar ham for sale in San Gimignano

horrific *Last Judgement* by Taddeo di Bartolo, showing the damned being punished in Hell.
Piazza del Duomo. Open: daily, 8.30am–12.30pm and 3pm–6pm. Admission free (except for the Santa Fina chapel).

MUSEO CIVICO

This museum is situated in the Palazzo del Popolo, itself a fine medieval building, part of which is still used as local government offices. Its main room is the Sala di Dante, so called because Dante, as the ambassador of Florence, delivered a speech here in 1299 arguing the case for Guelf unity. The walls have 13th- and 14th-century frescos.

On the left of the main staircase a plain little room contains two famous frescos depicting domestic life. Known as the 'Wedding Frescos', they show the bride and groom taking a bath together and in bed. In the adjoining picture gallery a painting of San Gimignano, the town's patron saint, shows him holding a model of the town in his hands; the painting dates from the late 14th century and shows how little San Gimignano's appearance has altered since. The staircase continues up the Torre Grossa, the highest of the town's surviving towers and the only one open to the public. Needless to say, there are splendid views from the top.
Piazza del Duomo. Open: April to September, 9.30am–12.30pm and 3.30pm–6.30pm; October to March, 9.30am–12.30pm and 2.30pm–5.30pm. Closed Monday in winter. Admission charge.

ROCCA

Little remains of this 14th-century castle but the interior has been been turned into a pleasant public park and there are superb views from the walls over the surrounding countryside.
Behind the Collegiata. Open: 24 hours.

SANT'AGOSTINO

This huge 13th-century church hides a treasure of Renaissance painting just behind the high altar. This is Benozzo Gozzoli's *Life of Saint Augustine*, in which scenes from the saint's life are illustrated in contemporary (15th-century) terms.
Piazza Sant'Agostino. Open: daily, 7am–12.30pm and 3.30pm–6.30pm. Admission free.

COMBINED TICKET
You can buy a combined ticket that admits you to all the sights in San Gimignano at any of the participating churches and museums. The ticket comes with a useful map of the town and a guide to its historic and artistic highlights.

San Gimignano Country Walk

This walk through the countryside around San Gimignano is especially pleasant in the autumn when the vineyards around the town are full of ripe grapes. *Allow 3 hours for the main walk or 1½ hours for the shorter alternative.*

MAIN WALK

Leave San Gimignano by the Porta San Matteo. Follow Via Garibaldi to the right, beneath the high walls surrounding San Gimignano. After 100m take the first left, then shortly afterwards turn right, taking the road that leads north towards Casale and Sant'Andrea. Beware of heavy traffic along the first stretch of this route, but do stop to look back at the incredible skyline of San Gimignano with the towers apparently springing straight up from the vineyards.

After 1km you will come to a junction with a little rural church on the right. Take the right-hand turning to walk along an unmetalled road signposted to Villa Pietrafitta. There is virtually no traffic along this track so you can walk at leisure,

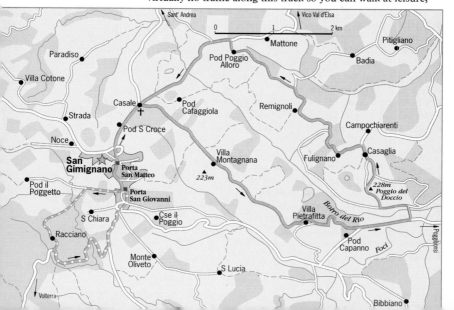

San Gimignano's sculptural beauty is best seen from the nearby vineyards

once again admiring the tremendous views over the valley to the right. Prominent in these views are the vineyards that surround San Gimignano, famous for their Vernaccia wine, a crisp dry white.

Villa Pietrafitta is reached after 3.5km. Continue through the hamlet for another 750m until you join the main road linking San Gimignano to Poggibonsi. Follow this road leftward (towards Poggibonsi) for just under 1km, then take the first left downhill and over a bridge across the Botro del Rio (the Rio Ravine). On the other side of the bridge turn left and then, after 500m, turn right to climb the hill called Poggio del Doccio (228m). Near the crest of the hill the road forks – take the right-hand branch through Casaglia. At the far side of this hamlet, the road branches again – turn left and follow the twisting rural road that runs along the northeastern side of the Vergaia valley. After 3km you will meet the main San Gimignano to Vico Val d'Elsa road. Turn left and follow this all the way uphill to San Gimignano, once again taking care because of the traffic.

SHORTER ROUTE

For a quicker introduction to the countryside, leave San Gimignano by the Porta San Giovanni. Turn right immediately outside the gate and cross to the car park to the right of Viale dei Fossi. Take the steep downhill track that runs down by the side of the car park. This will take you, within a couple of minutes, into beautiful open country with a dramatic backward view of the town. Continue down the road until it terminates in a farmyard after just over 1km. Take the left fork here to follow a rough farm track for about 2km. The track then joins a metalled lane – bear left and continue up the hill, where you will reach the large wine farm of Racciano after 250m. The road now runs along the crest of the hill for another 250m, providing wide views on each side, then plunges down through the vineyards. In autumn, just before the *vendemmia* (harvest), when the vines are heavy with fruit, this is a particularly attractive walk. The lane now joins the main road to Volterra. Turn left and follow the road up hill. After 2km you will regain the Porta San Giovanni.

Siena

*A*t almost every point, Siena is the opposite of its great Tuscan rival, Florence. Where Florentine buildings are classically inspired and built of brown or grey stone, Siena's are Gothic and built of reddish-brown brick, the colour known to artists as 'burnt siena'. Where Florence is dòur and masculine, its streets bustling with nervous activity, Siena is graceful and feminine.

Looking round this exquisite little hilltop city, with its population of 60,000 (as opposed to Florence's half a million), it is hard to realise that, in the Middle Ages, Siena fought it out on equal terms with Florence, with the balance more than once tipping in her favour. Gradually, however, the sheer

The Campo, the huge sloping square at the heart of Siena

power and wealth of Florence, the sheer cunning and skill of its politicians wore down its rival.

The final battle took place in 1555 and it has been estimated that Siena lost 60 per cent of its population in this last long and bloody contest. Having conquered Siena, the Medici Dukes covered it with their boastful insignia and then pursued a deliberate policy of suppressing Sienese business and

initiative. Siena did not die, for it has a tremendous inner vitality, but it did become a backwater for nearly four centuries.

Siena is built on six hills and this means that parts of it have the curious trick of appearing and disappearing like a city in some fairy tale. Some viewpoints will unexpectedly present Siena's dramatic skyline in its entirety while from others you can catch refreshing glimpses of open country. Siena's streets are much narrower than those of Florence and they are arched over in many places, creating a tunnel-like effect; even so, there is no feeling of claustrophobia and the vista is constantly changing.

Location: Siena is 68km south of Florence. Getting there: there are trains roughly every hour to Siena from Florence via Empoli. There is also a fast and regular bus service between Florence and Siena. Tourist information: Via di Citta 43.

BATTISTERO (BAPTISTERY).
Unusually for Tuscany, Siena's Baptistery is not a separate building. It is located at the east end of the cathedral, where the crypt would normally be, with a separate entrance at ground level, emphasising the steepness of the hill on which the whole structure is built. The Baptistery's supreme work of art is the great font. Florence and Siena might have been deadly political rivals but in

the freemasonry of art they did not hesitate to employ each other's great artists, and both Ghiberti and Donatello contributed to the sculptures on the font. *Piazza San Giovanni. Open: November to mid-March, 7.30am–1.30pm and 2.30pm–sunset; mid-March to September, 7.30am–7.30pm; October, 7.30am–6.30pm. Admission free.*

IL CAMPO

Completed by the year 1349 – just a year after the Black Death struck Tuscany – this vast shell-shaped piazza is the very heart of Siena and one of the most perfect public squares in all Italy. The Campo is paved in the same harmonious reddish-brown brick as the city's medieval buildings and it slopes downwards, forming a kind of ampitheatre with the Palazzo Pubblico as the stage. It is surrounded by buildings on all sides; access to the Campo is through narrow arched alleys so that visually the square looks completely enclosed. The only monument in the piazza itself is the Fonte Gaia. This is a copy (made in 1868) of the original fountain that was carved between 1408 and 1419 by Siena's greatest sculptor, Jacopo della Quercia. The remains of the badly eroded original panels are now displayed on the loggia of the Palazzo Pubblico.

SIENA TOWN PLAN

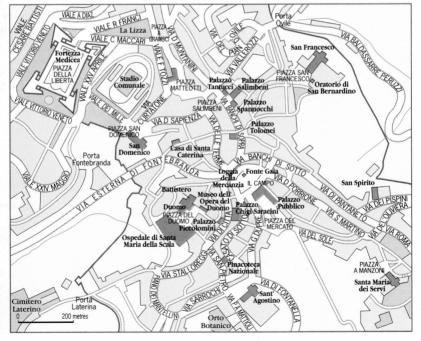

Duomo (Cathedral)

*T*he interior of Italian cathedrals tend to be somewhat bare, but Siena's is an exception. In fact, it is so crammed with interest that the best thing to do is to drop in for half an hour or so at a time – the generous opening hours make this possible. The interior is very dark so you will need a good supply of L200 and L500 coins for the automatic lights.

The cathedral is a vast building, but not big enough for the tastes of the Sienese who had no sooner completed this great building than they decided they wanted a bigger one. Work was started on a new structure but was brought to a halt by the Black Death of 1348. The enormous walls on the right-hand side (south) of the cathedral square is all that was completed of this ambitious project.

The striking black and white stripes of the cathedral's exterior is continued into the interior, to dazzling effect. Ranged high up around the nave is the most bizarre feature of even this remarkable building – polychrome busts of every pope who had ever reigned from St Peter up to the mid-16th century.

Of far greater artistic merit is Nicola Pisano's superb pulpit. Completed in 1268, it is similar to his great pulpit in Pisa's Baptistery with pillars supported by lions and dramatic relief sculptures.

The marble pavement of the nave is a unique and extraordinarily detailed work. Created between 1369 and 1547, it is said that every artist active in the city worked on these pictures at some stage. There are 56 scenes in all, ranging from simple black and white outlines to complex multi-coloured pictures in marble. In order to protect them, the cathedral authorities have covered some with hardboard, but some of the more interesting scenes are simply roped off. These include the elaborate *Massacre of the Innocents* scene near Pisano's pulpit and the fascinating black and white *Allegory of Fortune* by Pinturicchio, located in the centre of the nave; nobody knows the precise meaning of some of the scenes portrayed in this allegory, but that does not make it any the less enjoyable. The whole of the pavement is uncovered between 15 August and 15 September.

Siena's zebra-striped cathedral

POPE PIUS II

Aeneas Silvius Piccolomini was born in 1405 and came from a rich Sienese banking family. He travelled widely throughout Europe as a papal emissary, and then became both secretary and court poet to the Holy Roman Emperor, Frederick III of Germany. He became a priest quite late in life, was made bishop of Trieste and then, in 1456, appointed a cardinal. Two years later, in 1458, he was elected Pope Pius II. During his six-year reign he made a great effort to introduce reforms into the church. In Tuscany he created the beautiful little Renaissance town of Pienza, an early example of a planned town. His letters are delightfully readable and provide an insight into the Renaissance papacy.

Pinturicchio's work appears again in full glory in the *Libreria Piccolomini* whose entrance is on the left-hand (north) side of the nave. Here you can enjoy one of the most complete and beautiful displays of Renaissance painting to come from the hands of one man. The library was built in 1495 to house the books collected by the learned pope and humanist, Pius II. In 10 great panels painted in vibrant and luminous colour, Pinturicchio has illustrated scenes from the life of the pope, including his visit to James II of Scotland, his canonisation of Siena's own saint, Catherine, and the last, sad event of his life when he waited in vain at Ancona for the ships of the Christian powers who had promised to join his crusade against the Turks.

Heroes and saints look down from the Loggia della Mercanzia's ceiling

Piazza del Duomo. Cathedral: open summer, 7.30am–7.30pm; winter: 7.30am–1.30pm and 2.30pm–sunset. Admission free.
Library: open summer, 9am–7pm; winter, 10am–1pm and 2.30pm–5pm. Admission charge.

FORTE DI SANTA BARBARA
The great fortress that dominates the western approach to Siena was built in 1560 by Duke Cosimo I, and is one of several castles he had constructed to hold down the cities he conquered. Today the garden within the castle walls forms a pleasant and shady retreat. The bastion facing into the gardens of La Lizza houses a wine bar and shop called the Enoteca Italiana, with an immense stock from all over Italy (open daily, 3pm–midnight). The landscaped path running along the top of the castle walls provides excellent views of the city.
Entrance on La Lizza. Open: 24 hours. Admission free.

LOGGIA DELLA MERCANZIA
Situated where the three main streets of central Siena meet, this was a natural spot for merchants to gather. The *loggia* was built in the early 15th century and has recently been restored.
Via Banchi di Sotto.

MUSEO DELL'OPERA DEL DUOMO (CATHEDRAL WORKS MUSEUM)
This museum is housed in the bricked-up aisle to the right (south) of the Duomo, thus occupying part of the new cathedral that was planned but never finished. The ground floor is occupied by displays of 13th- and 14th-century statuary taken down from the façade of the cathedral. They include work by

Giovanni Pisano and Siena's own Jacopo della Quercia. On the first floor is the Sala di Duccio in which the work of Siena's greatest artist, Duccio di Buoninsegna, is displayed in an almost religious atmosphere of low lighting and hushed voices. Pride of place, in a blaze of gold, is given to the great *Maesta* – the Enthroned Virgin – completed in 1311. Opposite it are scenes from the *Life of Christ*, also by Duccio. These lively vignettes dispel the idea that early Sienese art lacks humour and realism. In *Peter Denying Christ* a group of men huddle round a fire in the cold small hours while a servant girl points accusingly at Peter, who holds up his hand in denial.

In the rooms above are further works of art, including the so-called *Madonna degli Occhi Grossi* (Madonna of the Big Eyes), painted in 1210 in the formal Byzantine style from which Gothic art developed. In the same room is an extraordinary reliquary with the skull and bones of some anonymous saint tied up with ribbons like a Christmas parcel. From the Sala dei Parati, where vestments are displayed, a small door leads to a staircase and viewpoint high up on the unfinished façade of the planned new cathedral. From here there are superb views of the cathedral roofs and of the countryside stretching south of Siena.

Piazza del Duomo. Open: summer, 9am–7.30pm; winter, 9am–1pm. Admission charge.

PALAZZO CHIGI-SARACINI

Like the Piccolomini, the Chigi were one of the great banking families of Siena with a foothold in the papacy. Their handsome 14th-century palace is now the seat of the highly regarded

musical academy, the Accademia Musicale Chigiana. The palace is not normally open to the public but you can walk into the beautiful inner courtyard with its splendid statue of Pope Julius III. On display there is usually a list of the concerts sponsored by the Academy. *Via di Citta 89 (tel: 0577 46152).*

Virgin and Child in Siena's Museo dell'Opera del Duomo

PALAZZO PICCOLOMINI

This is the most important of the three palaces which the Piccolomini pope, Pius II, built for his family in the city (the palace he built for his sister, irreverently known as the Palazzo delle Papesse – the Palace of the She-pope – is opposite the Palazzo Chigi). This palazzo is the work of the Florentine architect, Bernardo Rossellino, who also designed the city of Pienza for the pope. Today the palace houses the state archives. The great interest here is the series of painted wooden covers used to bind the city's medieval account books, the *Biccherna* and the *Gabelle*, which are works of art in their own right. They are exhibited in the Sala di Congresso, which is open to the public.

Via Banchi di Sotto 52. Open: Monday to Saturday, 9am–1pm. Closed Sunday. Admission free.

PALAZZO PUBBLICO

Siena's majestic city hall forms the
perfect centrepiece of the city's majestic
piazza, known simply as Il Campo – 'the
field'. Completed in the 1340s, the
building was so admired that it
influenced the design of all the other
buildings around the piazza, as well as

Even ordinary life seems more colourful in
historic Siena

buildings all over Siena. The incredible
campanile, known as the Torre di
Mangia, is the second tallest in Italy and
rises to 102m. The climb to the top is
well worth the effort because of the
stupendous views that open out. At the
base of the tower is the Cappella di
Piazza, a small chapel built in 1352–76
in the form of an open loggia in
thanksgiving for the end of the Black
Death.

As with most of Italy's historic city
halls, the Palazzo Pubblico is still the
centre of local government, but its main
historic rooms now serve as the city's
Museo Civico. The displays consist
largely of *in situ* frescos and they should
not on any account be missed because
they sum up, in dramatic and
understandable form, vital periods in
Italian history.

The museum is approached up a
modern steel staircase, past a well-run
museum shop, but then immediately
takes you back into the past. The ceiling
and walls of the first room are painted
with scenes illustrating key moments in
the *Risorgimento* – the long and often
bitter struggle that finally led to Italy
achieving unification in 1870. The major
figures depicted here are Garibaldi and
Vittorio Emanuele II, the first king of
modern Italy. The next important room
is the Sala del Mappamondo where
restoration of the great *Maestà* by Simone
Martini is in progress; while the original
picture is enshrouded in scaffolding, a
full-size colour photograph of the
painting is on display. On the opposite
wall is another great fresco, showing the
condottiero (mercenary), Guidoriccio da
Fogliano, setting off for battle in his full
military regalia. Beyond, in the Sala dei
Nove (Room of the Nine) are the
Allegories of Good and Bad Government by
Ambrogio Lorenzetti. Commissioned in
1338, these were intended to remind
Siena's governing Council of Nine, who
used the room for their meetings, of the
consequences of their decisions. *Good
Government* is shown as a resolute,
bearded figure flanked and supported by
all the Virtues while the citizens of Siena
happily go about their daily affairs. The
fresco presents a marvellous picture of
ordinary life in the 14th century. *Bad
Government* is characterised by the figure
of Fear presiding over a ruined
countryside where murder, robbery and
rape run riot.

*Piazza del Campo. Museo: open winter,
9.30am–1.45pm; summer, 9.30am–
7.45pm; Sunday, 9.30am–1.45pm.
Admission charge.*

*Torre di Mangia. Open varying hours from
10am. Separate admission charge to
museum.*

PINACOTECA NAZIONALE

The pictures in this art gallery demonstrate how Sienese art developed along different lines from that of Florence. Artists of the Sienese school were renowned for their delicate and mystical religious paintings, many of them depicting the Virgin, patron saint of the city, as can be seen by the many altarpieces exhibited on the first floor.

In Room 2 there are some lively little panel pictures from the 13th century whose very crudity of detail is attractive. Among them, for instance, is _The Story of Four Saints_ showing a strange obsession with torture. Highlights of the collection include the _Adoration of the Magi_ by Bartolo di Fredi (1330–1410) showing a contemporary view of Siena, and the portrait of the Borgia pope Calixtus III by Sano di Pietro (1406–81), which also has Siena as the background. The top floor of the gallery houses the Collezione Spannocchi, an important collection of small paintings by non-Italian artists, including Dürer's _St Jerome_ and a number of Flemish works.

Via San Pietro 29. Open: summer, 8.30am–7pm; winter, 8.30am–2pm. Closed Monday, Sunday and holidays.

Siena's Torre di Mangia campanile, the second tallest in Italy

Siena Town Walk

This walk runs right across the city, from one gate to another. It shows just how small is Siena for, walking briskly and without stopping, you could cross the entire city in 20 minutes. Of course, you will want to take longer because of the numerous distractions along the route. *Allow 1 hour.*

Start at the Porta Fontebranda.

1 PORTA FONTEBRANDA

Just outside this gate there is a good view of the city wall as it climbs the hill. The 14th-century wall still completely encircles Siena, a remarkable construction as it climbs and dips around the crests of the hills on which Siena is built. The Porta Fontebranda takes its name from the immense covered fountain a short way up the street. Built in the 13th century, it was so important and well-known that Dante made reference to it in the *Divine Comedy*. Towering above it to the left is the immense basilica of San Domenico. A little further up on the left, in Via di Santa Caterina, a short flight of steps leads to the Casa di Santa Caterina, the house in which St Catherine of Siena was born, now part of a convent.

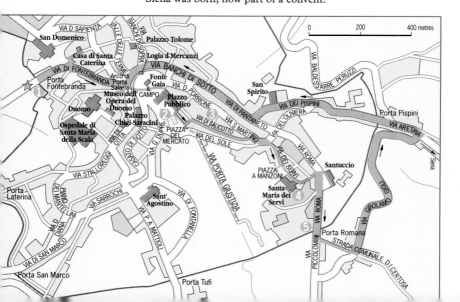

Return to the Porta Fontebranda and, with
your back to the fountain, head up Via di
Fontebranda, then cross the Via de Citta,
pass under the Arco di Porta Salaria and
enter the Campo (see page 113). Keep to
the right-hand side of the Campo, following
the façade of the Palazzo Pubblico and turn
right, beside the Torre del Mangia, into Via
de Salicotto. Take the first right, down Via
di Peschieri, and so enter the Piazza del
Mercato.

2 PIAZZA DEL MERCATO
This square is the setting for a pleasantly
bustling fruit and vegetable market.
If you would like the experience of a country
walk in the heart of a city, take the steps
which lead down from this southern end of
the Piazza del Mercato and follow Via
Porta Giustizia, a narrow lane which runs
along the valley. Otherwise, turn left out of
Piazza del Mercato, along Via dei
Malcontenti, thus returning to Via de
Salicotto, where you turn right.

3 VIA DE SALICOTTO
A few metres along you will come to a
dramatic example of local patriotism, a
terrace decorated with modern sculpture
and the Elephant and Castle statue of
the Torre (Tower) contrada, one of the
city's ancient parishes. The contrada has
a little museum at number 76 (ring for
the custodian).
At the next road junction turn right and
follow Via dei Servi, which leads to a quiet,
tree-lined square fronting the church of
Santa Maria dei Servi.

4 SANTA MARIA DEI SERVI
Climb the steps of this church for a
stupendous view of Siena's skyline.
Santa Maria contains notable paintings
such as the rather horrific Massacre of the
Innocents by Pietro Lorenzetti.

On leaving the church, turn right (north)
and look out for the plaque on the house
where Garibaldi was a guest as you descend
into a pleasant tree-lined road which leads
to Via Roma. Turn right here for the Porta
Romana.

The she-wolf, symbol of one of the
17 Sienese *contrade*

5 PORTA ROMANA
Almost every Italian city has a 'Roman
Gate' suggesting that all roads do,
indeed, lead to Rome. This gate is a
vast, roofless structure in pink brick with
a marble bench all the way round. Look
for the Medici balls which proclaim that
Siena was once ruled by Florence.
Tucked into one of its vast walls is the
office where licences are issued to those
few Sienese who are allowed to take
vehicles into the city.
You can either turn back here or, if you
have the energy, continue on through the
Porta Romana and take the road
immediately to the left, the Strada
Comunale di Certosa. After 100m turn left
along Via Girolamo Gigli. This runs for
400m through a mixture of countryside and
suburb roughly parallel to the city wall. It
leads to the Porta Pispini where you enter
the city again, following Via dei Pispini
back towards the city centre.

Florence to Greve in Chianti

Starting from the turmoil of the bus station in Florence this tour will take you along the romantically named Chiantigiana (the Chianti Way), passing through the quiet towns and villages of Chianti to Greve, one of the main towns in this little empire of wine. There are frequent bus departures from Florence to Greve (at least two an hour). This is also an attractive route for the motorist or even the cyclist – the distance involved is about 30km – though the hills are steep. *Allow 1 hour by bus.*

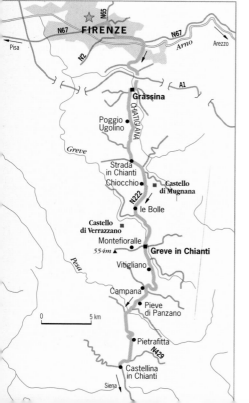

Florence has developed relatively little to the south so as you leave the city on the N222 you will quickly gain open country. You will pass under the A1 (the great Autostrade del Sole linking Milan to Rome, which also acts as a bypass for Florence) just before Grassina. From this point on, the N222 really does live up to its name, the Chiantigiana, as it ascends a ridge with wide views of typical Chianti landscapes on each side (for golf addicts the manicured lawns of Ugolino, Florence's golf club, is on the right just beyond Grassina).

Strada in Chianti is the next main stop along the road. The name Strada, meaning highway, is thought to date back to the Roman era and suggests that today's N222 follows the course of a Roman road. Not far away, the immense Castello di Mugnana stands guard over the road. This is one of the region's best preserved medieval castles; today it stands at the core of a big wine estate. If you are travelling by car or bicycle you can stop off here or at any of the other numerous *fattorie*, or wine farms, which line the route. Look out for notices on the side of the road saying Vendita Diretta – many offer free tastings, but having sampled the wine, you are expected to make a purchase.

Beyond Strada the road begins to descend rapidly towards Greve in Chianti. The pretty little town is an important centre for the prestigious Chianti wine trade. Like many of its neighbours, it holds a wine festival every September when the entire town centre takes on a festive mood. The core of the town is the splendid triangular market place, the Piazza Matteotti. The buildings on all three sides are fronted by colonnades with balconies above that, in summer, are ablaze with flowers. Shaded by the colonnades there are numerous small (and rather expensive) shops; as you would expect, many specialise in the wines of the Chianti region, while others specialise in *cinghiale* (wild boar) in various forms – such as delicious hams and sausages.

In the centre of the piazza is a handsome statue of Giovanni da Verrazzano, a 16th-century explorer who is credited with being the first European to visit the North American coastline where New York would one day be built. He was born in the Castello di Verrazzano, about 4km away, which sells a wide range of wines and olive oils.

If you are travelling by car or bicycle you can continue down the N222 all the way to Siena, calling at Castellina in Chianti along the route. Like San Gimignano, this hilltop town owes its picturesque appearance to the bitter necessities of medieval warfare. Castellina stood on the border between Florentine and Sienese territory and

controlled the junction of the region's three main roads. That accounts for its stout encircling walls, which are almost intact, together with the well-restored castle at the heart of the town, and one of its more unusual attractions – the extraordinary gallery or covered walkway, called the Via delle Volte, built as part of the 15th-century defences.

Radda in Chianti, surrounded by vineyards

The Versilia
(The Tuscan Riviera)

*T*he Italian seaside tends to arouse strong feelings among non-Italians. Accustomed to the idea that access to the beaches and the sea is one of the few free pleasures left in the world, visitors are startled to find that this is not always the case in Italian resorts. Flying in to Pisa airport, you will have a good view of the so-called Tuscan Riviera. It stretches from Marina di Carrara in the north all the way down to Livorno, a distance of some 60km, and nearly the whole of this seafront is lined by bathing establishments.

This long coastline is known as the Versilia, and it consists of eight towns, the largest of which is Viareggio. Most of the towns are located several kilometres inland from the sea but they all have a beach area known as a marina. The layout of each marina is identical, with hotels, restaurants, cafés and shops selling beach toys all set within a strict grid pattern of streets.

Beach Facilities

Once you get to the beach you will find that some parts are free; these are marked *Spiaggia Pubblica*. Most of the beach, however, will have been developed as a bathing establishment which will either belong to a nearby hotel or be operated by a commercial company. Such establishments, called *stabilimenti*, usually consist of a connected range of bathing cabins arranged around a central fountain or flower garden. The entrance fee covers the hire of one of these cabins for four people and the use of umbrellas and lounge chairs; there is sure to be a bar or restaurant within arms' length as well. The beach itself will be wide, safe and impeccably clean, perfect for young children to play upon.

VIAREGGIO

Although the towns of the Versilia appear to run into each other on the map, each has its individual core and good tourist information facilities. Viareggio is undoubtedly the pearl of the Versilia. Its street plan displays the same relentless grid pattern but a high proportion of the development consists of private houses with small front gardens. These, along with the the tree-lined roads and squares, make up a pleasant green town.

Viareggio also has a port area where, mixed among the luxury yachts, you can see tramp steamers and fishing boats. Local housewives and restaurateurs come to the port to buy their fish straight off the boat. From the end of the immensely long quay there is a superb view of the whole Tuscan Riviera stretching northwards, with the Apuan Alps (Alpi Apuane) forming a majestic backdrop.

The long, seafront promenade called the Viale Regina Margherita is an example of good town planning for the route is broken up at regular intervals by green squares and shady trees. Towards the port area, the buildings lining this promenade break out into cheerful art nouveau extravaganza. Doyen of them all is the Gran Caffé Margherita with its extraordinary cupolas covered with colourful ceramic tiles in a vaguely Persian style and a proud notice stating that Puccini and his friends frequently dined there.

Viareggio is a good base for excursions up and down the coast and into the hinterland. The main tourist information office, at Viale Carducci 10 (tel: 0584 48881/2), provides an excellent free guide book entitled *Itineraries for Tourists* which details 19 tours in the area that can be undertaken either by car, bus, or on foot.

VIAREGGIO TOWN PLAN

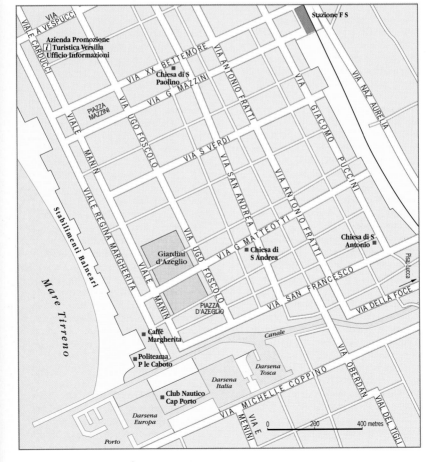

Volterra

*T*his rather eerie city, situated on a windswept plateau at over 500m above sea level, is one of the oldest, continually inhabited cities in Italy. The Etruscans established a settlement on this natural citadel around 800BC and there is evidence of even earlier occupation. The Etruscan city, called Velathri, became one of the most powerful in the Dodecapolis, the 12 city alliance. Present-day Volterra occupies only about a third of the area of ancient Velathri.

One of the most interesting ways to approach the city is from the north or the east; as you climb towards Volterra you will see the towering *balze*, dramatic precipices caused by landslips that are slowly eating away at the Etruscan circuit of walls. The bleak surrounding countryside is rich in minerals, including alum and alabaster. Alum was once the source of the city's wealth but also of its downfall, for Florence laid violent hands upon the city in 1361, determined to control the supply of alum, an important ingredient in the dyeing of cloth. Alabaster mining was revived in the 19th century and today forms Volterra's major industry.

The city is full of shops selling everything from exquisitely worked sculptures to table lamps and bowls worked in this marble-like stone.

DUOMO (CATHEDRAL)

For all its modest appearance Volterra's cathedral, begun in the 13th century, contains some interesting details: the great pulpit is in Pisan Romanesque style with lively sculptures, while the chapel in the right-hand (south) transept has a startling 13th-century *Deposition* carved in wood and painted in brilliant colours.

Piazza del Duomo. Open: daily, 8am–1pm and 4pm–7pm. Admission free.

MUSEO ETRUSCO GUARNACCI

This is one of the most important museums of Etruscan art in Italy. The collection consists of more than 600 funerary urns designed to hold the cremated remains of the deceased and made of carved alabaster, travertine or terracotta. The urns were all unearthed from ancient Etruscan cemeteries around the city. The bas-reliefs on the urns tell us a great deal about Etruscan life and beliefs; some urns are carved with domestic scenes, while others depict the mythology of the Underworld. One of the most famous urns is the so-called Urna degli Sposi (the Married Couple Urn). It is a startling example of realistic portraiture, depicting the rather coarse-featured couple 'warts and all'. Equally renowned is the mysterious, elongated bronze figure known as the 'Shadow of the Night', discovered in 1879 and used as a firepoker until experts realised this was a masterpiece of Etruscan art.

Open: summer, daily, 9.30am–1pm and 3pm–6.30pm; winter, daily, 8am–2pm. Admission charge.

PARCO ARCHEOLOGICO

This small park occupies the site of the ancient Etruscan acropolis and dotted around the grounds are the remains of temple foundations and Roman cisterns.

The ancient Etruscan Porto all'Arco greets visitors to Volterra

Towering over the park is the Fortezza Medicea, a well-preserved fortress completed in 1492 and still in use today as a prison.
Via di Castello. Open: during daylight hours. Admission free.

PIAZZA DEI PRIORI

This characterful square stands at the heart of the medieval city. Its centrepiece, the Palazzo dei Priori, is probably the oldest town hall in Tuscany. Begun in 1208, it established the pattern followed by Florence and many other cities. Opposite is the 13th-century Palazzo Pretorio with its cheerful Torre del Porcellino, taking its name from the little piglet carved on the base. On the right-hand side of the square is the showroom of the local alabaster-carving co-operative, displaying the work of Volterra's artists

PINACOTECA (ART GALLERY)

This splendid new gallery opened in 1992 and is housed in a 15th-century palazzo designed by Antonio da Sangallo the Elder. The collection is small but contains several outstanding works, most notably Rosso Fiorentino's *Deposition*, a dramatic example of Mannerist painting renowned for its bold colouring.
Via dei Sarti. Open: summer, daily, 9.30am–1pm and 3pm–6pm; winter, daily, 9.30am–1pm. Admission charge.

PORTA ALL' ARCO

The actual arch is a Roman reconstruction but the lower courses of massive stone without mortar are pure Etruscan. So, too, are the three blackened heads over the arch, probably representing gods.

TEATRO ROMANO (ROMAN THEATRE)

Volterra's Roman theatre and baths lie just outside the walls to the north of the city. The theatre, which is still being excavated, is the best preserved in Tuscany. The best views are to be had from Via Lunga le Mura which, as the name suggests, follows the line of the medieval walls.

Hill Villages

*R*oman cities in Tuscany are nearly always located in the valleys and plains, but the ancient Etruscans, and their medieval descendants, preferred to build on hilltops where the chance of fending off an enemy attack was that much greater. The Tuscan landscape is dotted with such hilltop towns, many of them of great age. Here are some examples of the most characterful.

Typical Tuscan hilltop town

Artimino

Originally an Etruscan town, Artimino is now a tranquil walled village (22km west of Florence) with a population of under 300. There are superb views over the Tuscan countryside and on summer nights fireflies and nightingales make it an enchanted spot. Some of the stone used to build the 12th-century church of San Leonardo came from the nearby Etruscan cemetery of Pian di Rosello (look for road signs pointing to the cemetery where archaeological excavations were in progress until recently). Just above the town is a 16th-century Medici villa, originally built as a hunting lodge by Buontalenti for Duke Ferdinand I. It is known as the 'Villa of a Hundred Chimneys' because of its bristling roofline. A luxury hotel and restaurant adjoin the villa's grounds.

Montefioralle

This silent, inward-looking village (1.5km west of Greve in Chianti) resembles one great castle, so closely integrated are its tower houses, its encircling wall and its Romanesque churches.

Monteriggioni

Dante compared the giants who surround the ninth circle of hell in his *Inferno* to the 14 towers that still surround this perfect little walled village (located 15km northwest of Siena). The wall and towers were built in the early 13th century by Siena as a frontier post on the border between its territory and that of its northern enemy, Florence. Exploring Monteriggioni's tiny interior, you become aware of the reason why the Italians tend to call every settlement larger than a hamlet a *citta* (city); with its two proud piazzas and its Romanesque church, this really does feel more like a miniature city than a village.

The cobbled lanes of Montefioralle

GETTING AWAY FROM IT ALL

There are thousands, millions of utterly
secluded little nooks, though the land has been
under cultivation these thousands of years.

D H LAWRENCE
Etruscan Places (1932)

The theatrical gardens of the Villa Garzoni, in Collodi near Lucca

GARDENS

The Renaissance formal garden was almost invariably attached to a rural villa and was designed as an outdoor extension of the house, with staircases, avenues and 'rooms' delineated in box hedging. In time, gardens became ever more elaborate, decorated with statuary, grottoes, fountains and *giochi d'acqua* ('water games') – hidden jets which drenched the unsuspecting visitor. The following are some of the best examples of Renaissance gardens to be seen in Tuscany.

GIARDINO DI BOBOLI, FLORENCE

The Boboli Gardens were designed as an extension of the Pitti Palace (see page 54) and they were laid out from 1549, with additional details added over the next 60 years. Since the Pitti Palace was the home of Tuscany's 'royal family', Grand Duke Cosimo I and his wife Eleanora, the gardens were designed to show their power and splendour. In 1589, for example, to celebrate the marriage of their son, Ferdinando, the palace courtyard was flooded to create the setting for a mock naval battle using 18 galleons. The main flight of steps leading up through the garden brings you to an immense pool and statue of Neptune. The avenue of cypresses which descends from here leads to a charming water garden, the Isolotto. *Piazza de'Pitti (tel: 055 213 440). Open: 9am all year. Closed: November to February, 4.30pm; March and October, 5.30pm; April, May and September, 6.30pm: June to August, sunset. Admission charge.*

PALAZZO PICCOLOMINI, PIENZA

In 1459 Pius II decided to turn Corsignano, the village in which he was born, into a model town. Pienza is the result. In the main square of the tiny hilltop town, Pius II built himself a palace, the Palazzo Piccolomini, and behind this palace is what can only be described as a 'hanging garden'. The garden is not very large but its designer, Bernardo Rossellino, took full advantage of the dramatic site, a narrow shelf between the palace and the very edge of the steep hillside.

Piazza Pio II. Open: Tuesday to Sunday, 10am–12.30pm and 3pm–6pm. Closed Monday. Admission charge.

VILLA GARZONI, COLLODI

The Garzoni family bought the old castle of Collodi (15km east of Lucca) in the early 17th century and converted it into a magnificent villa. The garden was laid out in the baroque style in 1786 and is a famous example of the last, luscious flowering of the formal garden before the fashion for naturalistic landscape gardening took over. The garden is, in effect, an enormous stage set with its statuary, fountains, topiary and a dramatic series of staircase terraces cascading down the hillside away from the villa at its summit.

Open: summer, daily, 8am–sunset; winter, daily, 8am–4.30pm. Admission charge.

VILLA DELLA PETREIA AND VILLA DI CASTELLO

These two Medici villas in the northern suburbs of Florence stand almost next to each other and are easily reached by bus number 28a, b or c; buses leave every 15 minutes or so from the main bus station. The journey takes about 15 minutes and you need to get off as close as possible to Villa della Petreia, off Via Reginaldo Gialiani. Via della Petreia leads up to the 16th-century Villa della Petreia whose gardens are laid out with box hedges in geometric patterns enclosing flower beds. You can also wander through extensive wild woodland at the rear of the villa. Its close neighbour, the Villa di Castello, is well signposted. The garden was laid out for Cosimo I in 1541 and features a shell-encrusted grotto for which Giamologna made the naturalistic bronze birds now displayed in the Bargello (see page 30).

Both gardens are open: June to August, Tuesday to Saturday, 9am–7.30pm, but closing at dusk for the rest of the year; Sunday, 9am–1.30pm. Closed: Monday. Admission free.

Neptune in the Boboli Gardens

SPAS

An Italian characteristic, which has endured down the centuries, is the obsession with bathing and other forms of water therapy. The Romans were, of course, very fond of their baths and built them in every part of the world that they conquered, even at the chilly extremes of their empire.

The descendants of the Romans have continued the tradition, using the same word *terme* for the institution (the word 'spa', derived from the name of a town in Belgium, is never used in Italy).

The *terme* performs two separate but related functions. First there is the therapeutic. Italy has no higher number of hypochondriacs than any other country but the advertisements for the *terme* do suggest a rather gruesome preoccupation with disorders of the liver, bowels and bladder. Water cures are taken under medical supervision and range from immersion and steam inhalations to simple consumption of measured doses of mineral-rich aqueous liquid.

The other function of the *terme* is to supply relaxation and entertainment. Drinking water that tastes of sulphur and iron filings is not one of the greatest of gastronomic experiences and the promoters have gone to great trouble to create various distractions, ranging from concerts to sports, all of which take place in beautiful surroundings.

Tuscany is particularly well provided with *terme*, the following being the most popular.

BAGNI DI LUCCA

Situated about 25km north of Lucca this is said to be the oldest *terme* in continual use in Italy, on the strength that Countess Matilda, the 11th-century ruler of northern Tuscany, is known to have bathed in the town's warm springs. The *terme* is located in beautiful wooded countryside, set among hills along the rushing River Lima. It achieved its social prominence in the early 19th century when Napoleon's sister, Elisa Baciocchi, briefly the ruler of Lucca, presided over a glittering social world. Distinguished foreign visitors to Bagni di Lucca have included Montaigne, Byron, Heine and Shelley. Europe's first licenced casino opened here in 1837 and the original building still survives, though boarded up pending long-delayed restoration.

Rejuvenation, relaxation, indulging yourself in beautiful surroundings – all part of the cure at Montecatini Terme

CHIANCIANO TERME

The ancient Etruscans made use of these hot springs but the mineral-rich waters have only been exploited on any large scale since the 1940s. Unlike Bagni di Lucca, which still retains the atmosphere of the past, Chianciano is functional and crisply modern. It does, though, have the attraction of the historic old town of Chianciano just 2km from the *terme*, and there are several historic hilltop towns in the immediate vicinity, such as Montepulciano and Chiusi.

MONTECATINI TERME

This is the most upmarket of all the Tuscan *terme*, famous throughout Italy for its varied architecture and fine gardens. Montecatini itself is a bustling modern city on the main railway line between Lucca and Florence, while the Parco delle Terme, the site of the spa, forms a large green wedge to the north of the city. Dotted around the green lawns of the Parco are nine separate thermal establishments, each built over a spring. The oldest is the Tettuccio, known since at least the 14th century but not developed until the 18th century. Its architecture is also the most distinguished. A day ticket is expensive but for this you can drink and bath in the warm, salty waters in the most luxurious surroundings.

Hot springs occur naturally at Saturnia, in southern Tuscany

BARGA AND THE GARFAGNANA

Variety in the landscape is one of the great attractions of Tuscany. The Lucca plain, along with the Arno valley to the south, is flat and densely developed, yet, just a few miles to the north, you enter a totally different landscape of towering peaks, narrow valleys cloaked in woodland and tumbling rivers icy cold from melting snow. The River Serchio, along with its tributaries, the Lima and the Secca, have, over the millennia, cut a course through the high mountains that form the central feature of the region. Major roads follow these main valleys, but once you depart from the beaten track you will find a wild landscape whose peaks are dotted with tiny, ancient villages clustered around their mother churches.

BARGA AND THE GARFAGNANA

In recent years parts of the Garfagnana have been designated as a nature reserve, or Parco Naturale, while others have begun to be developed for sports such as hang-gliding and skiing. There are also many hiking trails and the landscape is so varied that, at one extreme it offers gentle strolls through flower-rich meadows and woodlands, while at the other the conditions would test an experienced mountaineer. To explore the region you really do need to have your own transport. There is a railway line that follows the Serchio valley from Lucca to Aulla, but the mountainous nature of the region means that some stations – Barga and Bagni di Lucca in particular – are some considerable way from the town itself. The LAZZI buses from Lucca will take you to Barga within an hour and Castelnuovo, the 'capital' of the Garfagnana region, in about an hour and a half.

BARGA

The little town of Barga sits on a hill over 400m above sea level and the terrace in front of the cathedral at the highest point in the town offers an exhilarating vista to the high peaks of the Alpi Apuane range. One can only marvel at the pertinacity of the inhabitants who built their imposing cathedral in the 9th century on this dizzying spot. There are splendid Romanesque carvings round the outside of the cathedral and the great tank of a pulpit, dating from the 13th century, is carved with scenes from the Life of Christ. There is a small archaeological museum to the north of the church, while the rest of the town winds and twists down the hillside, its narrow lanes all the more delightful for the absence of traffic.

CASTELNUOVO DI GARFANGANA

Perched at the confluence of the rivers Serchio and Secca, this friendly little mountain town is also a major centre for mountain sports. Trekking, mountain-bike rallies, horse-riding and hiking are all popular here. Although livelier than Barga this is a peaceful mountain town where you can eat well and rest quietly. *There are two information centres: the Associazione Pro-Loco, in the massive 14th-century fort (tel: 0583-62268) and Garfagnana Vacanze, in Piazza dell'Erbe, specialising in adventure holidays.*

Grotta del Vento (Cave of the Wind)
The Cave of the Wind, near

Castelnuovo, a centre for sports

Fornovolasco, 9km southwest of Barga, is part of a massive cave system located deep within the mountains of the Apuan Alps. Visitors are taken on guided tours, ranging between one and three hours. *Open: daily, from 1 April to 31 October. Admission charge. It is advisable to telephone beforehand (tel: 0583 722020). Warm clothing should be taken – no matter how hot the day, the subterranean depths of this cave system are icily cold.*

PARCO NATURALE DELLA MAREMMA

Designated as a nature reserve in June 1975, this great park stretches for some 20km northwards from the little fishing village of Talamone. Protection does not mean that the park area has become fossilised: rural industries still continue to thrive within it, but hunting is forbidden and cars are not allowed within the confines of the park.

Umbrella pines in the Maremma park

The relative difficulty of access is part of the park's attraction, for it is rarely crowded and the varied vegetation supports many different kinds of wildlife. From the end of the Roman era, when neglect led to the choking up of the region's drainage systems, the Maremma was a place to be avoided, its stagnant marshes a breeding ground for malarial mosquitoes. The locality did not even have a proper name; *maremma* simply means 'land by the sea'. Redraining and recolonisation of the marshes began in the 18th century under Grand Duke Pietro Leopoldo but the northern area of the park retains a number of undrained lagoons which can be explored by canoe and where the birdlife is very rich – herons, storks, stilts and even flamingos can be seen here, as well as many varieties of duck. The unploughed Maremma pasture is grazed by white cattle with fercious looking horns. They are herded by horse-borne *butteri*, Italy's own version of the cowboy, so skilled at their task that in the 19th century they actually competed in rodeos and defeated the legendary Buffalo Bill Cody and his team. Today, every August, American cowboys compete with the *butteri* in special shows put on in Alberese.

For those who want to explore the park in more detail, there are four waymarked trails (a map is provided when you buy your entrance permit). On the other hand, you may decide just to laze on the beaches, which are among the most attractive in Tuscany. For restaurants and hotels the little walled fishing village of Talamone, at the southern tip of the park, is ideal, and there is a huge choice of places to stay and eat further south in Orbetello.

It is not easy to get to the park without private transport. Six trains run daily from Siena to Grosseto, the nearest big city. Buses run on an irregular basis to Alberese, the park's headquarters. For times, check with Grosseto Tourist Office at Via Monterosa 206 (tel: 0564 454510), open Monday to Saturday, 8am–2pm; or the parks headquarters in Alberese (tel: 0564 407098). The approach by car is along the Via Aurelia taking the Rispecia exit about 6km south of Grosseto. The opening hours of the park are also deliberately restrictive: officially you can enter 9am–sunset on Wednesday, Saturday, Sunday and bank holidays. Entry permits must be bought from the ticket office in Alberese and the fee includes transportation by bus to Marina di Alberese, a stretch of fine beach, sheltered by parasol pines, with picnic facilities.

DIRECTORY

There is much happiness in people who are born where good wines are found.
LEONARDO DA VINCI

Shopping

*T*he regional pattern of Italian society, and its sturdily conservative traditions, come out clearly in manufacturing and retailing. Almost every town specialises in some locally manufactured product, whether it is ceramics in Siena or alabaster in Volterra. Even cosmopolitan Florence, which has international names such as Gucci, Valentino and Ferragamo side by side on the Via Tornabuoni, is as proud as any village of its leather products, made in the backstreet workshops of Santo Spirito and San Frediano.

Tuscany has few supermarkets; small shops are the norm and retailers usually have a direct link with manufacturers – which in their turn are frequently small enterprises. Thus the Italian tradition of individual craftmanship not only survives, it flourishes, and the quality is very high – although caution must be exercised when dealing with street traders. They react with amazing rapidity to new demands; stalls selling umbrellas will sprout up within minutes of the start of any downpour, but the umbrellas they sell will not last out the week.

Florentine leatherwork is top quality

The high quality of most products means that goods are not cheap. Haggling is definitely not an Italian custom, but, as the person serving you is very probably the owner of the shop (and very possibly related to the manufacturer), and so can make on-the-spot decisions, there is a certain flexibility in pricing. It does not hurt to ask for a discount (*sconto*) particularly if you are spending a lot of money with that shop.

Shopping hours

In general shop opening hours are from 9am to 1pm and from 3.30pm or 4pm to 7pm, although the bigger shops in Florence are now experimenting with all-day opening. Shops tend to put their shutters up earlier on Saturday afternoon (around 5pm or 5.30pm) and many do not open on Monday morning. Very few shops open on Sunday. All shops must, by law, close for one day a week in addition to Sunday – details of the closing day will be posted on the door. In big cities, such as Florence, Lucca, Pisa or Siena, there will be one late shopping night a week, often Thursday.

Value Added Tax

Tourists from countries outside the European Community can claim a rebate of IVA (the Italian version of Value Added Tax) on individual purchases in excess of L930,000. Stores that participate in this scheme will supply full details and provide you with the necessary documentation.

FLORENCE

Although Florence is overshadowed as a shopping centre by Milan and Rome, when it comes to pride in craftsmanship Florence is still in a class by itself. If you want to see craftsmen at work, simply wander round Piazza Santa Spirito or any of the other narrow streets of the Oltrarno, the part of Florence that stands on the south side of the river.

Antiques

The problem that faces the innocent abroad in Florence looking for antiques and works of art is well illustrated by the superb advertisement put out by **Antonio Frilli**, Via dei Fossi 26r, who specialise in both genuine antiques and reproductions in marble and bronze: it is nothing less than a full-scale replica of Ghiberti's Baptistery doors. Renaissance Florence was, after all, the place which invented the *bottega* (workshop) system whereby the master would outline the project but leave much of the details to his apprentices. The borderline between work of art and copy, between genuine and reproduction is not always clear, so if you are not an antiques expert, be wary of parting with large amounts of money.

Art paper

Giulio Giannini e Figlio, at Piazza Pitti 37r, makes and sells the marbled paper which has been a speciality of Florence for at least six centuries. **Cartoleria 'Il Parione'**, Via del

Antiques from near and far

Parione 10r, prides itself on selling 'the kind of paper you would expect to find in Michelangelo's home town'.

Books and prints

Florence maintains its compact with scholarship through a marvellous range of bookshops. For visitors who do not read Italian, the simply named **BM**, on the corner of Borgo Ognissanti and Piazza Goldoni, is indispensable for its range of guidebooks and local histories in various languages, but principally English. **Feltrinelli**, in Via Cavour 12-20r, also has an excellent foreign-language section.

Clothing

The upmarket shops are concentrated in Via Tornabuoni. **Gucci** still remains loyal to its roots at **Via Tornabuoni 73r and Salvatore Ferragamo** is firmly entrenched in the splendid Palazzo Spini-Ferrone (16r). **Armani 35-37r** has moved round the corner to Via della Vignaduova 51r.

Florence is home to several of the world's top fashion designers

Jewellery

Ever since Ferdinando I expelled the butchers, blacksmiths and tanners from the Ponte Vecchio in 1593, the bridge has been famous for its jewellers' shops. Do not be misled by the modest-looking shopfronts: the goods sold here can be expensive (although you can also buy very modestly priced trinkets). At least you know that the goods sold in these shops as gold really are gold – unlike the 'genuine gold jewellery' sold at remarkably low prices by peddlers on the bridge. Away from the Ponte Vecchio you may find the prices less hyped. **Ugo Piccini** has an elegant shop

in the base of a tower at Via Por Santa Maria 9/11r which specialises in watches and jewellery. **Bijoux Cascio**, Via Par Santa Maria 1r, specialises in costume jerwellery – big chunky gold-plated pieces at affordable prices.

Leather

Leather goods are sold virtually everywhere in Florence, from the stalls in Piazza San Lorenzo market, where identical belts are hung in their hundreds (cheap but good) to the elegance of the **Bottega Fiorentina** at Borgo de' Greci 5. The latter is set in a palazza with a delightful courtyard and fountain.

OUTSIDE FLORENCE

AREZZO
The Piazza Grande is a good place to shop for antiques and reproductions. The entire piazza is given over to an antiques fair on the first Sunday of every month.

MONTEPULCIANO
The **Azienda Agraria**, Via San Donato, is a farm co-operative selling honey and wax products (including soap made from honey) and the knee-buckling liqueur called Aquavita di Montepulciano. **Ramela Mazzetti,** near by on Via San Donato 15a, sells copper utensils, new and antique.

PIETRASANTA
Pietrasanta (the name literally means 'Holy Stone') is located on the coast, 18km south of Carrara, and appropriately enough specialises in marble goods. To see typical products, go to the **Consorzio Prodotti Artistici de Marmo (CAMP)**, on Viale Marconi 5. This syndicate brings together more than 50 manufacturers specialising in marble, onyx, bronze, mosaic and ceramics. CAMP can handle everything from the manufacture of a ceremonial marble staircase to a simple candlestick.

SAN GIMIGNANO
San Gimignano is a delightful place to shop, with the two main streets, Via San Matteo and Via San Giovanni, lined with scores of speciality outlets selling everything from modern art (ceramics, paintings and sculptures) to typically Tuscan foods, wines, olive oils and liqueurs. Several shops also sell the local white wine, Vernaccua di San Gimignano, and the tourist office sells posters of local sights.

Vini e salumi – wines and sausages

SIENA
Sena Vetus: Antichita, Via di Citta 53, is an antique shop which tempts you to come in and browse among the artfully casual display. For books, the nearby **Libreria Senese**, Via di Citta 66, stocks everything from scholarly monographs to science fiction in several foreign languages as well as Italian; the shop is also excellent for local maps and guides and has a mezzanine gallery with a stunning range of children's books.

For ceramics, one of Siena's specialities, try **Neri: Ceramiche Santa Catherina**, Via di Citta 51. This has a glittering display of traditional designs and there is usually someone in the shop working on a design, bearing out the proudly displayed claim *Produzione Propria* (hand made).

Another fascinating shop in the same street is **Stampe Cornici Bianchi**, Via di Citta 112, which sells historic and modern posters, with a particularly interesting range illustrating the Palio (see page 150).

MARKETS

Every day in summer the little town of Pescia, some 27km east of Lucca, bursts into multi-coloured bloom. This is Italy's largest flower market, with over 1,000 growers selling millions of flowers to hundreds of florists from all over Europe. Many of these flowers are grown in the surrounding countryside, and the fields either side of the N435, between Lucca and Pescia, are a patchwork quilt of flower colours.

In Arezzo, the Piazza Grande is taken over on the first Sunday of every

month by a popular antiques fair. The products displayed on some stalls may challenge your idea of what constitutes an antique, but it is nevertheless fun to browse and occasionally take a gamble.

In Siena the feast of Santa Lucia, in December, is marked with a massive display of ceramics, one of the city's major art forms.

Florence boasts five general markets. The biggest is the Tuesday morning market in the Cascine Park, to the west of the city, where Florentines go to buy bargain-priced clothes and shoes. Another market takes over Piazza San Lorenzo, alongside San Lorenzo church, every day in the summer (not Sunday or Monday in

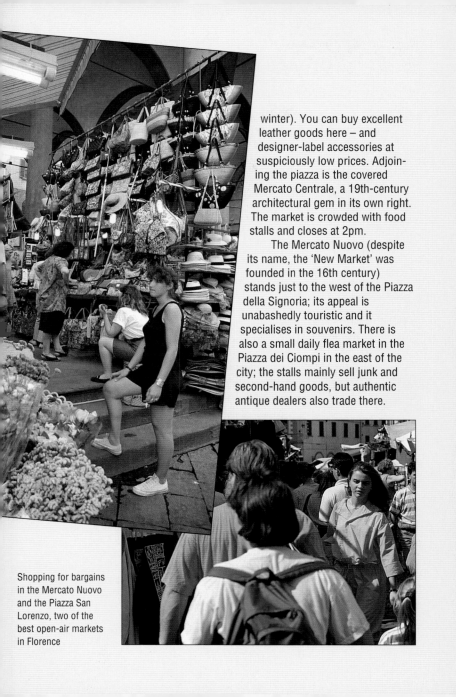

winter). You can buy excellent leather goods here – and designer-label accessories at suspiciously low prices. Adjoining the piazza is the covered Mercato Centrale, a 19th-century architectural gem in its own right. The market is crowded with food stalls and closes at 2pm.

The Mercato Nuovo (despite its name, the 'New Market' was founded in the 16th century) stands just to the west of the Piazza della Signoria; its appeal is unabashedly touristic and it specialises in souvenirs. There is also a small daily flea market in the Piazza dei Ciompi in the east of the city; the stalls mainly sell junk and second-hand goods, but authentic antique dealers also trade there.

Shopping for bargains in the Mercato Nuovo and the Piazza San Lorenzo, two of the best open-air markets in Florence

Entertainment

Big cities such as Florence, Siena and Pisa offer the best chance of enjoying professional entertainment. The student populations of these cities also ensure that there are discos to go to, although fashions change with bewildering rapidity.

Even in these big cities, however, Tuscans largely seek out the traditional and spontaneous forms of entertainment provided by human contact: the evening promenade, a leisurely meal with friends in a favourite restaurant, conversation over a glass of wine in a café or simply watching the world go by in the main piazza. It is no accident that, consciously or unconsciously, many an Italian square resembles a theatrical stage on which the comedy of human manners is played out nightly.

The Italian passion for music (and especially opera) is a boon for non-Italian speaking visitors. Even in the smallest cities there is bound to be a concert on somewhere during the week. In Florence, the major festival of classical music and opera, called the

Maggio Musicale Fiorentino, runs from May to July. Lucca puts on an ambitious opera season in the autumn, usually featuring one or more operas by Puccini, who was born in the city (see page 91). Opera is to Italy what ballet is to Russia and, apart from the superb music, it is staged with enormous panache. It does, however, tend to be rather expensive: around L20,000 for the cheapest seats.

Film is also extremely popular, and every town has a cinema (in summer, films are also shown in the open air, in the grounds of the Forte di Belvedere in Florence, for example). Many of the films shown in small-town cinemas are home-grown Italian products, but you may well find undubbed English language films being shown in larger cities.

Listings information can be found in the regional daily newspaper, *La Nazione*; though published in Florence, this carries local inserts for each of the nine provinces in Tuscany, including news of local events. The very useful English-language publication, *Florence: Concierge Information*, is available free at most

Some bars put on jazz or piano music in the evenings

hotels. *Firenze Spettacolo* is published monthly in Italian and is available at most bookstalls. The tourist boards of Siena and Pisa publish an annual calendar of events which is available free from the tourist offices. Siena also has a lively weekly arts publication, *La Voce del Campo*.

FLORENCE AND VICINITY

In recent years, partly in response to tourist demand, and partly out of a traditional love of spectacle, Florence has evolved a remarkable series of spontaneous street theatres. After the evening stroll, *passeggiata*, the Piazza della Signoria, the Piazza del Duomo and the street that links the two, Via Calzaiuoli, becomes a continuous stage occupied by different groups. Mime artists take over Piazza della Signoria and are watched by crowds of 100 or more. Via Calzaiuoli is lined with fortune tellers using computers and printers to give a high-tech gloss to their traditional methods. Musicians, both classical and pop, play to moderately sized audiences in the Piazza del Duomo.

Watching the sun go down from an open-air café in Florence

FLORENCE
Cafés, bars and discos
Andromeda, Via dei Cimatori 13 (tel: 055 292 002). 10pm till late. Closed Sunday. Admission charge.

Caffe Voltaire, Via della Scala 9r (tel: 055 218 255). Members only but reasonable joining fee. Closed Sunday.

Central Park, Via Fosso Macinante (tel: 055 332 723). 10pm till late.

Cobra Pub, Via Gobetti 1, (tel: 0574 21814). Open: 8pm till late. Closed Wednesday.

Energia, Via Silvestri 18, (tel: 0574 6070945). Open: 9pm till late. Closed Monday.

Eskimo, Via dei Canacci 12r (tel: 055 210 605). Open: 9.30pm–3am.

Jackie O, Via dell'Erta Canina 24 (tel: 055 234 2442). Closed Monday.

Meccano, Viale degli Olmi (tel: 055 331 371). Open: 8pm till late.

Montecarlo Club, Via dei Bardi 2 (tel: 055 234 0259).

Nelson Pub, Via M Nistri 51/53, (tel: 0574 42161). Open: 7pm till late. English-style.

Pura Vida, Piazza Umberto I, Grassina (tel: 055 64008). Restaurant with live music Thursday. Closed Wednesday.

Sahara Desert, Viale XXVII Agosto. Rap and reggae. Open: 10pm till late.

Space Electronic, Via Palazzuolo 37 (tel: 055 293 082). High tech with lasers. 8pm till late.

Stonehenge, Via dell'Amorino 16r. Rock. Open: 10pm–4am.

Teatro dell'Acqua, Lungarno Pecori Giraldi. Garden with river view. Open: 10am till late. Closed in the winter.

Tenax, Via Pratese 47, Peretola, near airport (tel: 055 373 050). Florence's biggest disco. Closed Monday and Tuesday.

Toro Loco, Via San Gallo 16r (tel: 055 295 244). Closed Monday. Flamenco dancing.

Cinemas
For a listing (in Italian) of all current films on show in Florence, tel 198. Among the many cinemas in the city are:

Alfieri Atelier, Via Ulivo 6 (tel: 055 240 720).

Astro, Piazza San Simone. English-language films.

Spazio Uno, Via del Sole 10 (tel: 055 283 389). Occasional English-language films.

Open-air cinemas
Arena Giardino Grotta, Viale Gramsci, 393 (tel: 055 446 600).

Pianta Cinema, Forte Belvedere, (tel: 055 234 1536).

Poggetto Cinema, Via M Mercati 24b (tel: 055 422 1754).

Music and Theatre
Amici della Musica, Via G Sirtori, 49 (tel: 055 608 420).
Orchestra della Toscana, Via dei Benci 20 (tel: 055 242 767).
Teatro Comunale, Corso Italia 16 (tel: 055 277 9236).
Teatro della Pergola, Via della Pergola 12 (tel: 055 247 9651/2).
Teatro Niccolini, Via Ricasoli 5 (tel: 055 213 282).
Teatro Verdi, Via Ghibellina 99 (tel: 055 239 6242).

PISA AND VICINITY
Cafés, bars and discos
Babalu, Via della Repubblica Pisan 64, Marina di Pisa (tel: 36877).
Babylon, Via Niccolini 5, Capannoli (tel: 0587 609 939).
Discoteca Imperiale, Largo Belvedere, Tirrenia (tel: 050 37673).
Divina Club, Via San Casciani 8 (tel: 050 43285).
Frumpy, Via Pisorno 64, Tirrenia (tel: 050 37650).
La Boite, Viale del Tirreno 22, Tirrenia (tel: 050 33280).
Gatto Verde, Via T Rook 13, Barbaricina.
Waikiki, Via Veneto 200, Pontedera (tel: 0587 55130).

Cinemas
Ariston, Via Turati 1 (tel: 050 43407).
Astra, Corso Italia 18 (tel: 050 23075).
Mignon, Lungarno Pacinotti 2 (tel: 050 24428).
Teatro Italia, Corso Italia 120 (tel: 050 41316)
Teatro Odeon, Piazza San Paolo all'Orto (tel: 050 540 168).

Music and theatre
Teatro di Pisa, Via Palestro 40 (tel:

050 541 864/542 434 or 542 476).
The theatre organises a wide range of programmes in historic sites in and around Pisa.
Teatro del Giglio, Piazza del Giglio, Lucca (tel: 0583 46147 or 47521).

SIENA AND VICINITY
Cafés, bars and discos
Al Cambio, Via Pantaneto 48 (tel: 0577 43183).
Gallery, Via Pantaneto 13 (tel: 0577 288 378).
L'Officina, Piazza del Sale 3 (tel: 0577 228 6301).

Cinemas
Cineforum Siena, Piazza dell'Abbadia 6 (tel: 0577 283 044).
Fiamma, Via Pantaneto 141 (tel: 0577 220503).
Impero, Viale Vittorio Emanuele II 14 (tel: 0577 48260).
Nuovo Pendula, Via San Quirico 13 (tel: 0577 43012).

Music and theatre
Accademia Musicale Chigiana, Via di Citta 89 (tel: 0577 46152).

Festivals and Events

Siena's Palio (see page 150) is so spectacular that it has overshadowed all other Tuscan festivals. Virtually every city has similar festivities, however, usually associated with a saint's day or with ancient rivalry between different parts of the city, and a distinctive feature of most of these festivals is that local participants dress the part, wearing splendid period costume.

The following is a selection of the most important festivals. Since the dates can vary, check with local tourist offices for further information.

Joust of the Saracen (Arezzo)

This medieval-style joust, held in August, begins with a colourful parade of townspeople in period costume who process to the Piazza Grande. There, eight horsemen, representing the old districts of the city, gallop at a dummy (called *il Saracino* , the Saracen) mounted on a swivel; the aim is to strike the centre of his shield, at the same time avoiding a blow from his whip as he spins round. The winning district is awarded a silver lance.

Feast of the Immaculate Conception (Bagni di Lucca)

This important feast day in the calendar of the Catholic church is celebrated by a fair in the Fornoli quarter.

Burning of the Tree (Camporgiano, near Lucca)

On Christmas Eve, 24 December, an immense bonfire of evergreen branches burns to the accompaniment of the great bell of San Giacomo.

Explosion of the Cart (Florence)

At noon on Easter Sunday a dove descends on a wire from the high altar of the cathedral and ignites a cart full of fireworks in the Piazza del Duomo. The ceremony is supposed to commemorate the First Crusade, when Crusaders brought back flints from the Holy Sepulchre in Jerusalem.

Cricket Festival (Florence)

This festival takes place on Ascension Day in Cascine Park. Floats are paraded and stallholders sell crickets in cages which are traditionally released in the park.

The Explosion of the Cart, Florence

Feast of San Paolino (Lucca)

A torchlight parade in period costume is held in July in honour of the city's patron saint. A crossbow contest is held in the evening, organised by the city's venerable Company of Crossbowmen.

Feast of Santa Croce (Lucca)

Another torchlight procession takes place in September, this time in honour of one of the most revered relics of the Middle Ages, the Volto Santo or Holy Face kept in the cathedral (see page 92). A fair is held on the following day.

Game of the Bridge (Pisa)

This game, held in June, involves two groups representing the two halves of the city. One on each side of the river Arno, they battle for possession of the Pont di Mezzo, Pisa's main bridge. They do this by trying to push a heavy cart, weighing 7 tonnes and sliding on rails, over to the opposing side.

Joust of the Bear (Pistoia)

This contest takes place in July when 12 riders, three from each quarter of the city, gallop with a lance and attempt to spear two targets in the form of bears.

Exposition of the Virgin's Girdle (Prato)

This precious relic is displayed to the faithful from Donatello's pulpit in the façade of the cathedral on several occasions during the year, namely Easter Sunday, 1 May, 15 August, 8 September and Christmas Day. On the Feast of San Stefano on 26 December Prato celebrates the feast of its patron saint, St Stephan.

Crossbow Contest (Sansepolcro)

This contest, held in September,

Festive Florentines in Renaissance costume

originated in a dispute between the crossbowmen of Sansepolcro (in Tuscany) and those of Gubbio (in Umbria) over which town had the better marksmen. Today's participants dress in period costume.

Feast of Santa Cecilia (Siena)

A varied programme of concerts takes place in November in honour of the patron saint of music.

Feast of San Giuseppe (Siena)

Donkey races, floats and tournaments in March.

Feast of Santa Lucia (Siena)

Ceremonies in the church of Santa Lucia followed by an outdoor pottery and ceramic fair, held in December.

Viareggio Carnival

One of Italy's biggest, lasting for nearly three weeks in February. Elaborate floats are paraded every Sunday.

THE SIENESE PALIO

The Palio is a bareback horse race, run in Siena each year on 2 July and 16 August, in which the prize is a *palio* or banner. The race has been run, practically without a break, at least since the 13th century. Originally it took the form of a wild helter skelter gallop through the city, but in the 16th century the race was transferred to the city's main square, the Piazza del Campo. The race is still hazardous, for although the pavement of the piazza is sanded and buffers are placed between the course and the crowds of spectators, the circuit involves negotiating the steep slope of the piazza and its acute angles.

Palio in Siena – a celebration of local patriotism

The dangers to horse and rider merely add to the thrill of the most spectacular of all Tuscany's traditional festivities, and that most vividly presents the strong Tuscan sense of local patriotism. The race is run by representatives of 10 out of the 17 *contrade* or parishes of Siena. Seven of the 10 consist of those who did not compete in the previous Palio, while the other three are drawn by lot. The horses, too, are allocated to the riders by drawing lots, and it is the horse, not the rider that is most important: under the strange (some would say non-existent) rules, it is quite possible for a riderless horse to win the race if it shows sufficient flair in the process.

After the lots have been drawn, representatives of the *contrade* lead their horses away, keeping them under close guard, knowing that their rivals will attempt to nobble the horse. Six trial races are run before the Palio itself. This takes place in the evening and is

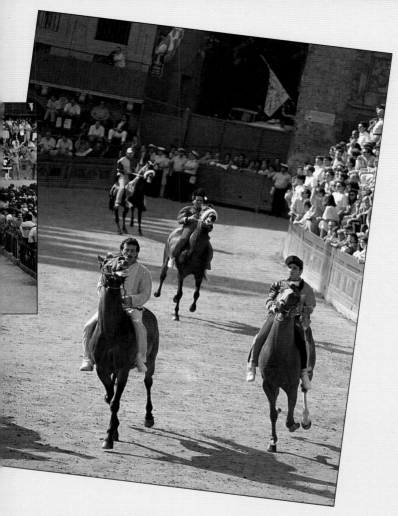

preceded by a stirring ceremonial display put on by the *contrade*. The riders, along with many of their wildly enthusiastic supporters, all dress in medieval costumes, featuring the colours of their *contrada*. Onlookers crowd the centre of the square, as well as the windows, balconies and roofs of the surrounding buildings, and it is certainly no place for the claustrophobic. After a year's preparation, the whole race is over in about 90 seconds, the time it takes to make three circuits of the piazza. The inhabitants of the winning *contrada*, delirious with delight, than embark on a round of celebrations which can continue for weeks.

Children

*T*he fact that Italians adore children, and – given the opportunity – spoil them outrageously, goes a long way towards making a family holiday in Italy a happy experience. There is no need to worry whether or not you are allowed to bring your child into a café or bar: it is assumed that a parent naturally knows best when and where to take a child. Even in large cities, local children follow the lead set by their parents and use the city's streets and squares as a playground and stage – under mamma's watchful eye – drawing in visiting children to the freemasonry of childhood. It is fascinating to see how rapidly small children, without a word of each others language, can establish a dialogue based on mutual curiosity.

The very attractions which draw their parents to Tuscany, however – the works of art, the architecture, the bustling cities – can be purgatory for the young. For them, the prime attraction of Tuscany will probably be the seaside and, happily, the Versilia coast (see page 124) is, in effect, one vast and safe playground.

Puppets for sale at the Pinocchio theme park in Collodi

FLORENCE
Florence has a number of entertainments specifically geared to children aged six to 14. Known as *Ludotece,* they are a sort of cross between play school, with group activities, and theatre, with spectator events. Among them are:
La Carozza di Hans, Via Modigliani 102 (tel: 787 7734). Open 9am-1pm and 3pm-7pm. Closed Wednesday, Saturday afternoon and Sunday.
Ludoteca Centrale, Piazza Santissima Annunziata 13 (tel: 247 8386). Open 9am-1pm and 3pm-7pm. Closed Wednesday and Saturday afternoon.
Ludoteca Magicaluna, Via A da Settimello 92 (tel: 882 053). Open Monday, Wednesday and Saturday, 3.30pm-6.30pm.
Con Te: da zero a tre (for children aged up to three but parents are also welcome), Via U Foscolo 39 (tel: 420 1075). Open Monday to Friday, 10am-12 noon and 3pm-6pm. For current activities see the *Citta e Ragazzi* pages of *Firenze Spettacolo.*

PINOCCHIO THEME PARK
Another favourite attraction among young visitors to Tuscany is the **Parco**

was the custodian of the splendid Villa Garzoni (see page 131). Fond memories of his childhood led Lorenzini to adopt Collodi as his pen name and Collodi, the town, returned the favour by creating this theme park in the 1950s.

The park is located right in the centre of the town and is open daily, 8.30am to sunset (tel: 0572 429342). You should allow at least half a day to enjoy its attractions; there is an excellent restaurant and good picnic facilities. Although it is obviously designed with children in mind, adults too can enjoy the sculptures that dot the grounds, produced by some of Italy's foremost artists.

Having fun in Florence and making friends with the city's bronze boar

di Pinocchio at Collodi, located about 15km east of Lucca. The Pinocchio of this theme park is not to be confused with the bland confection served up by Walt Disney. The book *The Adventures of Pinocchio* has, for Italians, the same significance as *Alice in Wonderland* has for the British or *Huckleberry Finn* for Americans. Pinocchio's creator, Carlo Lorenzini (1826-90), was born in Florence but he spent much of his childhood in Collodi where his uncle

Sport

*I*t is a debatable point whether sport or music comes first in the affections of many Italians. In Florence, love of sport led the city to commission the great architect Pier Luigi Nervi (who built the Audience Hall in the Vatican) to create the Stadio Comunale in 1932 – a remarkable modern building recently used to host part of the World Cup.

Quite apart from spectator sport, Tuscany's mountains, rivers, bridlepaths and coastline offer plenty of opportunity for active participation in a number of sports.

CYCLING

Walk into any bar in Tuscany on a Saturday afternoon and the chances are

that if the television is not tuned into a football match, then it will be covering a cycle race. The northern Italians love this gruelling sport and a lot of sponsorship money is poured into supporting top cyclists! If you want more information, the best place to look is in the sports pages of the local papers, but you can also contact the following branches of the organisation that controls the sport, the Federazione Ciclistica Italiana, Piazza Stazione 2, Firenze (tel: 055 283 926) or Via Pastore 3, Cenaia, Pisa (tel: 050 643 652).

GOLF

Golf Club	Holes	Location	Phone
Acquabona	9	Portoferraio	0565 804 309
Casentino	9	Poppi	0575 520 167
Cosmopolitan	18	Tirrenia	050 808 8456
Florence Ugolino	18	Grassina	055 2301 009
Fontevivo	3	San Miniato	0337 703 515
Golf Range	2	Lucca	0583 979 750
Hermitage	9	Portoferraio	0565 969 932
Le Pavoniere	18	Prato	0574 620 855
Montecatini	9	Monsummano	0572 62218
Punta Ala	18	Punta Ala	0564 922 121
Tirrenia	9	Tirrenia	050 37518
Versilia	18	Pietrasanta	0584 881 574

FISHING

Tuscany's rivers – in their upper reaches at least – are clean and offer lively sport to anglers. There are also scores of small lakes and rivers that are deliberately stocked with fish – some so tame that they will eat out of your hand. To fish anywhere in the region you need an annual permit. This is very cheap and can be obtained from offices of the Federazione Italiana della Pesca Sportira. There are branches of this organisation in every provincial capital in Tuscany (just ask at the local tourist office) or you can go to the office in Florence at Via de'Neri 6, 50122 Firenze (tel: 055 214 073). As well as issuing permits, the organisation will provide you with advice and information on fishing times and places.

FOOTBALL

If you are wandering around the Campo dei Miracoli in Pisa on a Saturday afternoon during the Football season, your thoughts on the asethetic beauty of the Leaning Tower and the cathedral are likely to be rudely interrupted by the

Fishing below Castelnuovo di Garfagnana

roaring, singing and chanting of football supporters, watching a game in the massive stadium that stands just to the north of the city walls. Football is as popular in Tuscany today as gladiatorial combats were in ancient Rome – the difference is that the crowds are far more good natured and the violence that mars the sport in some parts of Europe is not a feature of the Italian game. Posters are put up all over town (look in bars and on shop doors) giving the details of the forthcoming fixtures and you can watch the game by simply turning up and paying at the turn stile. Tuscany's top team is the Florentine side, Fiorentina, which has won the Italian league in the recent past but is now considered rather mediocre. They play at the Stadio Comunale, part of the huge sports complex on the Campo di Marte on the eastern edge of the city. Other teams to watch are the first-division side Pisa and the two second-division sides, Empoli and Lucca.

HORSE RIDING

Riding and trekking are very popular in Tuscany (and even more so in neighbouring Umbria) so there is no shortage of opportunities to take a riding holiday. Quite a number of rural hotels

offer riding as an option and will make all the necessary arrangements for you. Alternatively, you can contact ANTE (the National Association for Equestrian Tourism) at Largo Messico 13, Roma

for further information, or visit any of the following riding clubs:

Florence
Country Riding Club, Via di Grioli, Badia Settimo, Scandicci (tel: 050 790 277).
Badia Montescalari, Figline Val d'Arno (tel: 050 959 596).

Pisa
Alfea Mensa Artieri, Viale delle Cascine 149 (tel: 050 533 281).
Associazione Ippica Pisana, Vione dei Porcari 2, Tirrenia (tel: 050 32268).
Centro Equitazione e Turismo Equestre, Via Roma, località La Certosa, Calci (tel: 050 938 447).

Siena
Club Ippico Senese, localita Pian del Lago (tel: 0577 318 677).

An altogether more ambitious programme is provided by the Communita Montana della Garfagnana (tel: 0583 658 990). This consists of a waymarked horseback trail through the mountains of the Garfagnana region, stopping overnight at 16 staging posts, each of which offers lodgings, a restaurant and stabling.

HORSE RACING
Florence
For information on race meetings in Cascine Park contact Centro Ippico Toscano le Cascine, Via Vespucci 5 (tel: 055 372621).

Pisa
San Rossore (tel: 050 531 132).

Siena
Ippodromo, Pian delle Fornaci SS Loc
Costalpino (tel: 0577 394347).

HUNTING
This is a highly emotional subject in
Italy. The opening of the hunting season
in September is signalled by a deafening
fusillade of shots spoiling the peace of the
Tuscan countryside. Locals complain
bitterly about town dwellers, dressed as if
for guerrilla warfare and with an
alarmingly casual attitude towards their
lethal weapons, virtually laying siege to
isolated farmhouses and hamlets whose
terrified inhabitants dare not walk in their
own fields for fear of stray shots. Since
the start of the hunting season coincides
with the grape harvest, when scores of
people are spread out among, and
partially concealed by, the grape vines,
there is further ground for accidents and
for conflict between locals and incoming
hunters. The Italian government is also

Rowing the Arno beneath the bridges of Florence

uneasily aware of Italy's bad international
reputation for blasting migratory
songbirds out of the sky; increasing
restrictions on hunting are being applied,
but frequently they are ignored.

Having said that, there are rigorous
restrictions concerning the import of
firearms into the country. The
Federazione Caccia (Hunting
Federation) at Via Crispi 49, Pisa (tel:
050 20331) is a useful contact. Visiting
would-be hunters are also well advised to
consult the most authoritive source
before planning their holiday. This is the
Federazione Italiana Caccia, Via C Da
Ancona 27, Roma (tel: 06 575 0117).

ROWING
For rowing on the Arno in Florence
contact the Canottieri Firenze Comunali
Lungarno Ferrucci 6 (tel: 055 681
2151). The more upmarket Societa
Canottieri Firenze has a delightful
clubhouse and landing stage near the
Ponte Vecchio at Lungarno de' AML
Medici 8 (tel: 055 282 130). In Pisa
contact the La Federazione Italiana
Nuoto, Canoa e Canottaggio, Via
Mazzini 138, Pisa (tel: 050 500870).

SCUBA DIVING AND UNDERWATER FISHING

Special permits are issued by the provincial Harbour Master's office. Only people over 16 are allowed to use underwater guns and similar equipment. When submerged, an underwater fisherman is required to indicate the fact with a float bearing a red flag with a yellow diagonal stripe and must operate within a radius of 50m of the support barge or the float bearing the flag. Fishing is prohibited under 50m from a beach used by bathers or from fishing installations or ships at anchor. Further information from the SCUBA Federation, Via R Fucini 49, Pisa (tel: 050 540 190).

SPORTS AND FITNESS CENTRES

Florence

Farfalla, Via Montebello 46 (tel: 055 296 040).
Gymnasium, Via Palazzuolo 49 (tel: 055 293 308).
Manfredini, Via Cavour 106 (tel: 055 588 302).
My Center, Via dei Bardi 104 (tel: 055 234 2801).
My Club Fitness Centre, Via P Mascagni 11 (tel: 055 891 545).
Palestra Savasana, Via Jacopo da Diacceto 26 (tel: 055 287 373).
La Palestra, Via La Farina 50 (tel: 055 247 6363).

Pisa

Aerobic Holiday, Via Emilia 43 (tel: 050 983 208).
Alhambra, Via Fermi 27 (tel: 050 29111).
Athletic Club, Via A della Spiona 11 (tel: 050 500 888).
Body Centre, Via Corridoni 110 (tel: 050 500 408).

Eucaliptus Centro Fisico Culturale, Via Pindemonte 2 (tel: 050 576 449).
New World Gym Club, Via Garibaldi 177 (tel: 050 575 616). Men only.
Olympia, Via Cisanello 121a (tel: 050 575 946).
World Gym Club, Via Colombo 40 (tel: 050 25145). Women only.

Siena

Centro Turistico Studentesco Giovanile, Via Angiolieri 49 (tel: 0577 285 008).
Centro Universitario Sportivi, Via L Banchi 3 (tel: 0577 52341).
Mens Sana, Viale A Scalvo (tel: 0577 47298).
Vertus, Via Vivaldi (tel: 0577 221 055).

SWIMMING

Virtually the entire Tuscan coastline has sea-bathing facilities, but of varying quality. The most developed area lies between Marina di Pisa and Marina di Carrara (see page 124). Most towns also have at least one open-air swimming pool (*piscina*) and the major ones are listed below.

Florence has three pools that are open from June to September. The most popular is in Cascine Park – the **Piscina le Pavoniere** (tel: 055 367 506). The **Piscina Bellariva** is at Lungarno Colombo 6 (tel: 055 677 521), and the **Piscina Costoli** is at Viale Paoli (tel: 055 669 744).

Pisa has two pools: **Piscina Comunale** at Via A Pisano (tel: 050 532 582) and **Piscina San Giuliano**, at Via del Brennero (tel: 050 81705).

Siena also has two: **Piscina Comunale**, Piazza G Amendola (tel: 0577 47496) and **Piscina Quattro Querce**, Strada di Marciano 31 (tel: 0577 40013).

TENNIS

Florence: **Circolo Tennis alle Cascine**
(tel: 050 356 651).
Pisa: **Federazione Tennis**, Via F
Melani 3 (tel: 055 574 110).
Siena: **Circolo Tennis La Rachetta**,
Via Vivaldi 2 (tel: 055 221 100).

TREKKING

Trekking in Tuscany is becoming very
popular and there are several specialist
firms that specialise in walking holidays.
One of them is the **Amiata Impianto e
Turismo**, Via della Pace 68, Abbadia
San Salvatore, Siena (tel: 0577 776 421).
Founded in 1989 by trekking enthusiasts,
this organisation now organises a range
of sporting holidays in Tuscany,
including skiing, mountain-biking and
canoeing. Whatever your level of
accomplishment, the cooperative can
work out itineraries to suit.

For independent travellers an
extremely useful publication is the
*Annuario delle Strutture Ricettive della
Toscana*. This comprehensive guide
contains suggested itineraries and
schematic maps, with advice on the best
local maps to buy. There is also a free
leaflet, *Trekking in Toscana*, published by
Regione Toscana Servizio Promozione
Turistica e Sport, Via di Novoli 26,
Firenze (tel: 055 438 3823), which is also
obtainable from provincial tourist offices.
The leaflet describes 10 trekking
itineraries with details of the best maps to
buy, information on public transport and
the addresses and telephone numbers of
information offices along the route.

WINTERSPORTS

Tuscany's main wintersports resort is at
Abetone, on the border with Emilia
Romagna and some 50km north of
Pistoia. This is also one of the best ski

The wide and slow flowing Arno at Pisa

resorts in Italy, much favoured by
wealthy visitors, with good hotels and
restaurants, numerous ski-lifts up to the
slopes and splendid mountain scenery.
This makes it just as popular in summer
and many of the hotels do popular and
inexpensive packages: the so-called
Settimare Bianche (White Week)
packages include the cost of a room, all
meals and ski passes, and the Settimare
Verdi (Green Week) packages offer
accommodation, meals, trekking, tennis
and swimming in the summer months.
Packages are easily booked through
travel agents and further information on
wintersports generally can be obtained
from the Federazione Italiana Sport
Invernali, Viale Matteotti 15, 50121
Firenze (tel: 055 576 987).

Food and Drink

For Italians, food is part of an important social and aesthetic experience – that is one of the reasons why everything closes down for the lunch hour which actually lasts for the whole afternoon. Junk food is virtually unknown, except in the larger cities, and fast-food chains such as McDonald's and Wimpey are few and far between. Even in modest little restaraunts, meals are served with a certain style and the food is almost invariably excellent.

A typical Tuscan *alimentari* or grocery shop

Prices and charges

Prices are perfectly fair and vary according to the type of establishment. In an average restaurant you can expect to pay L20,000 a head for your meal. In addition you will find extra charges for service (usually 15 per cent) and *pane e coperto* (literally 'bread and tablecloth') of up to L2000 per person; for this you should get a basket full of fresh bread,

but you may be charged again if you order extra bread.

Many restaurants serve *prezzo fisso* (fixed price) meals, costing from around L12,000 to L20,000. This usually consists of a choice of first course (soup or pasta), a choice of main course dishes (often plainly roasted pork, lamb or chicken) served with a vegetable or salad, plus fruit or cheese. Some restaurants also include a bottle of mineral water or a 250cl carafe of table wine and the price includes both service and cover charges. In up-market restaurants the customer is expected to order a full three (or even four) course meal. In humbler establishments you can order just one dish (a plate of pasta, say).

Picnic food

If you want to eat cheaply, especially at lunchtime, a pleasant alternative to eating in a restaurant is to create a picnic from the delicacies sold at an *alimentari* (grocer's shop). Grocers sell an incredible range of pickled, preserved and cured foods. Apart from the ubiquitous salami, you could sample artichoke hearts (*carciofi*), smoked boar (*cinghiale*), roast quail (*quaglia*), anchovies (*acciughe*) and many other savoury treats. The measure for this kind of food is the *etto* (*uno etto* – one etto – is 100gm, sufficient for two or three people). With bread, fruit, cheese and a bottle of wine you could build up an excellent picnic for two for around L20,000. Do remember to do your shopping before 1pm, however, as most *alimentari* close at this time and do not open again until 3.30pm or later.

Cheap eats

Another inexpensive alternative, to be found in most towns of any size, is the *tavola calda* (literally 'hot table'), a self-service restaurant where the cover and service charges are included in the clearly displayed price of each dish. You can either choose a single item, such as a plate of *lasagne*, or you can have a complete meal.

Of course, to many people Italy is synonymous with pizza and, within Tuscany itself, this relatively humble dish is undergoing something of a revival – Florence and Siena both have excellent *pizzeria* specialising in the genuine article, cooked in a wood-fired oven. Various kinds of wood, including chestnut, olive and grape vine, are used to fire the pizza oven, and the gentle smoky fragrance adds something extra even to the plainest pizza.

OIL AND WINE

Oil and wine, along with bread, pasta, tomatoes and olives, are among the great staples of the Italian diet. In shops specialising in wine and oil (*vini e oli*) there may well be as wide a range of olive oils on offer as there are wines. Restaurants will boast that their oil comes from their own olive groves: others will offer you a choice, as they would a wine list. Tuscans, in short, treat olive oil seriously.

OIL QUALITY

Olive oil varies greatly in flavour from area to area even though the groves may be only a few kilometres apart. Like vintage wine, the best quality oils proudly state on the label exactly where they are fromr. The very finest quality, known as *Extra Vergine*, is that obtained from the first pressing and it has an acidity level of less than one per cent. After the first pressing, the mash is progressively heated to extract the remaining oil, but the quality deteriorates with each subsequent pressing.

ITALIAN WINES

Italy is the world's largest producer of wine, although the Italians rank just behind the French in actual consumption. Italian wines are not as popular overseas as French, not because they are inherently inferior but because their marketing has never been as good. This in itself reflects the immense rangè of wines produced, with every little village making its own local wine. Tuscany led the way in imposing

From Tuscany's vineyards and olive groves come fragrant oils and fruity wines

Chianti Classico wines bearing the
Gallo Nero (Black Cockerel)
quality symbol on the neck

some kind of order when, in 1924, a consortium of Chianti wine growers banded together to produce quality wine to a consistent formula proposed by one of the area's largest winegrowers, Barone Bettino Ricasoli. The consortium has since adopted the Gallo Nero (Black Cockerel) as its symbol, and this is now universally recognised as a sign of very drinkable, soft and fruity wine.

After World War II the Italian government instituted the DOC (Denomiazione d'Origine Controllata) system whereby the label had to state the place of origin of the wine. In 1966 San Gimignano, near Siena, became the first locality to adopt the DOC system for its delicious and crisp dry white Vernaccia wines. Many growers dislike government control and there are certainly many excellent wines that do not have the DOC label but it does help to give some guidance to the uninitiated.

ENOTECA ITALIANA

The best place in all of Italy – not just Tuscany – to get an idea of the range of Italian wines is the Enoteca Italiana in the Medici fortress in Siena (see page 116). The venue is itself is extremely attractive. You descend by a beautiful curving brick stair to the main showroom deep within the bastions of this 16th-century fortress. Here, arranged like precious objects in a jeweller's shop, the wines are grouped by their place of origin. Upstairs is a bar and another showroom frequently used for special exhibitions. A free booklet lists the 227 wines available. In the bar you can buy wine to sample either by the glass or by the bottle at very fair prices for a generous glass. For maximum pleasure, take your glass on to the terrace under the great wall of the castle and taste at your leisure, preferably as the sunset turns the sky and the rooftops of Siena a lovely roseate red. The Enoteca is open every day from 3pm to midnight (tel: 0577 288 497).

Italian Food

The three main meals of the day in Italy are *colazione, or prima colazione,* (breakfast), *pranzo* (lunch) and *cena* (dinner).

Colazione can be, for non-Italians, the least satisfactory of all, since many Italians are content to start their day with a thimbleful of strong black coffee and some kind of cake. If you are unable to face a sugary doughnut first thing in the morning, most bars also have a selection of savories, such as salami-filled rolls. If you want coffee made with milk ask for *caffe latte*; alternatively you can ask for *cappuccino* (so-called because the frothed-up milk poured on top of the coffee is the same colour as the cowl of a Capuccin monk)

Pranzo (lunch) is often the main meal of the day on Sunday and is served around 1pm. During the rest of the week, *cena* (dinner) is the main meal. Restaurants serve pretty much the same menu at lunch and in the evening. A full meal can consist of up to four courses with a bewildering range of choice,

Seafood *antipasti*

especially at the *antipasto* stage; the mouth-watering range of appetisers on offer may include salami in half a dozen forms, seafood served hot or cold and various pickled or preserved vegetables (in some restaurants, *antipasti* are frequently displayed on a table for you to serve yourself.

Next comes the *primo piatto* (first course); this consists of pasta, rice or soup in any one of 100 different varieties. The *secondo piatto* (main course) consists of meat or fish accompanied by a *contorno* (side dish) of vegetables or salad (side dishes are priced separately and are entirely optional. Last of all you can choose between fruit (*frutta*), cheese (*formaggio*) or a dessert (*dolce*).

If you want to try the local wine, you can ask for a quarter, half or litre carafe. *Vino da tavola* (table wine) is both good and cheap. Branded wine, even from the locality, is likely to be much more expensive.

Italy used to have two main types of restaurant, the *trattoria* and the *ristorante*. Originally the *trattoria* was a humbler family-run establishment. With increasing professionalisation of the catering trade, the *trattoria* has become increasingly hard to find – where they do exist, they still tend to be cheaper than the *ristorante*. An old name being revived is the *osteria* (hostelry). This can be confusing for visitors and natives alike; sometimes an *osteria* serves rustic and inexpensive food, while, at the other extreme, it can be a trendy, and quite expensive, restaurant.

Tuscan specialities

Tuscan food is, essentially, country food – hearty, chunky, and highly flavoured. An example of how it combines frugality with flavour is *bruschetta*, bread rubbed with garlic and brushed with olive oil, then toasted. Beans figure in a variety of forms and other Italians refer to Tuscans as *mangiafagioli* – the bean-eaters. *Fagiolini* consist of green beans, usually served cold with olive oil. *Fagioli* are white beans served with a variety of dressings. *Zuppa di fagioli* is bean soup. *Ribollita* (meaning 'reboiled') is solid soup cooked to the point that all the stock is absorbed into the bread and vegetables. *Zuppa di verdura* is a thick soup of green vegetables, such as cabbage.

Apart from these staples, almost every city has its own speciality. In Pisa you can get *ciechi alla pisani*, baby eels cooked in garlic and tomatoes (and of course a wide range of other fish dishes). Florence offers *bistecca alla fiorentina*, a massive steak brushed with olive oil and grilled over charcoal, and *trippa alla fiorentina*, strips of tripe braised in tomato sauce and garlic. In Lucca you get a superb *minestra di farro*, soup to

Fresh anchovies in lemon marinade

which grains of wheat are added. Arezzo offers *pappardelle alla lepre*, long flat pasta flavoured with hare sauce. Siena is renowned for *panforte*, a rich cake made of honey, nuts and fruit, originally made to sustain pilgrims on their journeys.

If you like good food, the best approach is to experiment: waiters are proud of their work and will do their best to describe the ingredients of any unfamiliar dish – which may well be unknown to Italians from other parts of the country as well as to you.

Eating out is a family occasion, an adventure to be enjoyed

Restaurants

The following price indications are based on the cost of a full meal per person, excluding drinks:

L   up to L20,000
LL   L20,000 to L40,000
LLL   L40,000 and above

FLORENCE

Antico Fattore L

You have to fight for service and a place at table but the food is cheap and good, honest Tuscan. *Via Lambertesca 1–3 (tel: 050 238 1215). Closed Sunday and Monday.*

Cantina Barbagianni LL

Attractive cellar bar restaurant with a varied menu and friendly service. *Via Sant'Egidio 13 (tel: 055 248 0508).*

Enoteca Pinchiorri LLL

Lavishly praised by all who use it as one of Italy's best restaurants, renowned for its amazing winelist. Garden courtyard for summer dining. *Via Ghibellina 87 (tel: 050 242 777). Closed all day Sunday and Monday lunch.*

Gauguin LLL

Elegant vegetarian restaurant serving an interesting menu. *Via Alfani 24/R (tel: 055 234 0616). Closed Sunday and Monday lunchtime.*

Il Giardino LL

Good Tuscan food with friendly service. Covered garden at the back, pleasant in summer. *Via della Scala 61/R (tel: 055 213 141).*

Hotel Excelsior LLL

There are two choices here, both sumptuous: either the Edwardian opulence of the ground-floor restaurant or the roof-terrace with its superb views of Florence. *Piazza Ognissanti 3 (tel: 050 264 201).*

Harry's Bar LLL

This a clone of the more famous bar in Venice and it serves American-style cocktails and burgers. *Lungarno A Vespucci (tel: 050 239 6700). Closed Sunday.*

Le Fonticine LL

Cosy and traditional, but sophisticated restaurant with an eye to the tourist trade. *Via Nazionale 79r (tel: 050 282 106). Closed Monday.*

La Grotta Guelfa L

Tucked away on a loggia just behind the Mercato Nuovo, this is one of the few places in the city centre where it is possible to eat cheaply in the open. Very popular with locals. *Via Pelliceria 5r (tel: 050 210 042). Closed Sunday.*

La Loggia LL

Restaurant with a view, high on the hill to the south of the city. *Piazzale Michelangelo (tel: 050 234 2832). Closed Wednesday.*

Il Mandarino LL

Chinese restaurant close to the Ponte Vecchio. *Via Condotta 17r: (tel: 050 239 6130). Closed Monday.*

Osteria Antico Mercato LL

Excellent Italian food in pleasant surroundings, close to the station. *Via Nazionale 78/R (tel: 055 284 182).*

Osteria del Cinghiale Bianco LL
Friendly and busy family trattoria south of the river (advisable to book). *Borgo San Jacopo 43/R (tel: 055 215 706).*

Palle d'Oro LL
Busy marketplace *trattoria* at lunchtime, cosy rustic atmosphere in the evening. *Via Sant'Antonino 43–45/R (tel: 055 288 383). Closed Sunday.*

Trattoria Angiolina LL
Situated in the narrow streets of the Oltrarno district south of the river, this is a traditional Florentine *trattoria* frequented by locals and a few knowledgable visitors. *Via Santo Spirito 36r (tel: 050 239 8976). Closed Monday.*

Trattoria Da Marino LL
Restaurant with an open-air terrace 'under the shadow of the cathedral Dome'. *Via della Cannonica 1r (tel: 050 210 285). Closed Monday.*

Trattoria Quattro Leoni LL
Set in a small, intimate square in the

Oltrarno district, this *trattoria* is a popular meeting place for artists. *Via dei Vellutini 1r (tel: 050 218 562).*

AREZZO
La Buca di San Francesco LL
Consciously arty but with good local food including *pappardelle alla lepre* (pasta with hare sauce). *Piazza Umberto 1 (tel: 0575 23271). Closed Monday evening and Tuesday.*

Logge Vasari LL
An ideal place for a leisurely lunch, looking out on to the Piazza Grande from the shade of Vasari's loggia. *Via Giorgio Vasari 19: (tel: 0575 25894).*

La Scaletta L
Rumbustious and cheerful, this is one of the cheapest places to eat in Arezzo. *Piazza del Popolo 11 (tel: 3537340). Closed Thursday.*

CARRARA
Ristorante Roma L
No menu but a range of excellent daily specials. *Piazza Cesare Battisti 1 (tel: 0585 70632). Closed Saturday.*

CASTELLINA IN CHIANTI
Ristorante Tenuta di Ricavo LL
Elegant but traditional Tuscan restaurant. *Located in a little hamlet 3km north of Castellina (tel: 0577 740 0221). Closed Monday and Thursday.*

GREVE IN CHIANTI
Bottega del Moro LL
Excellent and friendly restaurant specialising in regional dishes, such as *zuppa di funghi* – soup made from a variety of wild mushrooms. *Piazza Trieste 14r (tel: 055 853 753). Closed Monday.*

Da Verrazzano LL
Gourmet meals served on a terrace overlooking the main piazza. *Piazza Matteotti 28 (tel: 055 853 189). Closed Monday.*

LUCCA
Antica Locanda dell'Angelo LL
There has been an inn (*locanda*) on this site since at least 1414. First-class cuisine for which it is advisable to book. *Via Pescheria 21 (tel: 0583 47711). Closed Sunday evening and Monday.*

Il Buca di Sant'Antonio LL
An upmarket restaurant specialising in local cuisine. Booking advisable. *Via della Cervia 3 (tel: 0583:55881). Closed Sunday and Monday.*

Rusticanella 2 L
Cheap and cheerful and an excellent place for a quick bite of lunch. *Via San Paolino 32 (tel: 0583 55383). Closed Sunday.*

MONTECATINI TERME
Ristorante Marino LL
Situated near the station, ideal for a quick meal on arriving or leaving. *Corso Matteotti 151 (tel: 0572 73363).*

MONTEPULCIANO
Porta di Bacco Pulcino LL
The quality of food varies but the ambience, in a wine cellar (*enoteca*) is very enjoyable. *Via di Gracciano nel Corso 106 (tel: 0578 757 907).*

PISA
L'Artilafo LL
Small and intimate restaurant with lively atmosphere, complete with live music. *Via Volturono 38 (tel: 050 27010). Closed Wednesday.*

Banco della Berlina L
Specialising in local dishes at very reasonable prices. *Piazza Cairoli (tel: 050 542 716). Closed: Monday evenings.*

Da Francesco L
Tuscan cuisine and a garden. *Via Santa Maria 129 (tel: 050 45366). Closed Sunday.*

Il Krosto L
Set in one of Pisa's historic tower houses. *Via Mercanti 4 (tel: 050 542 655). Closed Sunday.*

La Tana L
Friendly, rambling and rumbustious tavola calda . *Via San Frediano 6 (tel: 050 580 540). Closed: Sunday and Saturday morning.*

Osteria del Violino LL
Medium-sized restaurant serving regional cuisine with a wine cellar attached. *Via la Tinta 25 (tel: 050 48410). Closed Sunday.*

Al Ristoro dei Vecchi Macelli LLL
Despite a somewhat off-putting name 'the Old Slaughterhouses' this is one of Pisa's most refined and upmarket restaurants. *Via Volturno 49 (tel: 050 20424). Closed: Wednesday.*

Taverna Kostas LL
Popular student restaurant serving Greek and Italian food. *Via del Borghetto 39 (tel: 050 571 467). Closed Wednesday.*

SAN GIMIGNANO
Dorando LLL
An extremely imaginative chef who specialises in researching and recreating classic Renaissance dishes – quite a feat of culinary archaeology. *Vicolo del Oro 2 (tel: 0577 941 862). Closed Monday.*

Enoteca il Castello LL

This *enoteca* (wine bar) is situated in a medieval palazzo and is outstanding for its service, its typically Tuscan specialities including *cinghiale* (wild boar), its wines and its ambience. Superb panoramic view from terrace. *Via del Castello 12 (tel: 0577 940 878).*

SIENA
Il Campo LLL

Extremely expensive – but then you are paying for a table beneath the stars on the famous Campo as well as for a gourmet meal. *Piazza Campo (tel: 0577 280725). Closed Tuesday.*

Nuove Donzelle LL

Like the hotel in which it is situated, this restaurant is popular with those tied to a strict budget. *Via delle Donzelle 1 (tel: 0577 42069). Closed Sunday.*

Osteria 'l Grattacielo' L

Tiny cabin on the corner of Via dei Pontani and Via dei Termi. No menu, communal tables and cold food only – but the locals queuing up to get in testify to the value. *Closed Sunday.*

Osteria Le Logge LL

Traditional *trattoria* serving gourmet dishes at good prices. *Via del Porrione 33 (tel: 0577 48013). Closed Sunday.*

Ristorante Da Renzo LL

Pleasant family-run restaurant with excellent table wine and a good 'fixed price' menu. *Via delle Terme 14 (tel: 0577 289 296). Closed Monday.*

LA VENEMMIA (THE HARVEST)

Two great harvests take place every year in Tuscany, that of the grapes and that of the olives. Grape vines and olive trees grow companionably side by side, flourishing in the same conditions of soil and sun. Their harvesting, however, takes place at different seasons.

The grape harvest begins in the second half of September and for about a month the villages and small towns are filled with the heady scent of the fermenting fruit. As recently as the 1990s it was possible to see oxen pulling immense wooden containers piled with grapes. Today, they have been superseded by noisy little tractors and trailers. The picking of the grapes, however, is still largely done by hand. This back-breaking and time-consuming process provides employment for casual labourers, including many students and young people from other parts of Europe or from as far afield as the USA and Australia. It is still possible to obtain such work, though wine growers are increasingly turning to mechanisation.

Not all of the grapes are pressed at once. A Tuscan speciality is *Vin Santo* (literally 'Holy Wine' – so called because priests are said to love it), made from grapes that are dried in the sun for about 10 days after picking. They then become more like raisins and the wine made from them is usually served as a dessert wine accompanied by sweet almond biscuits.

Olive trees grow to an immense age, and olive groves are handed down from one generation to another. The trees have to be pruned and manured every year to ensure that they will bear an abundance of fruit. The berries are usually left on the tree until they turn

black and harvested in December. They, too, are plucked by hand, the method being to shake or rake the berries from the tree, catching them in a net suspended beneath. Most of the crop is taken to a mill where they are processed commercially. Some villa estates still process their own crop and sell the product, specially packaged, at a premium price, though these days the pressing is done by machine and the traditional stone wheel, operated by a donkey or horse, is very much a thing of the past.

Hotels and Accommodation

HOTELS

Italian hotels are graded on a star system, the best hotels being awarded five stars and those with fewest facilities being awarded one. In general, a five-star hotel really does mean that you will receive five-star treatment – and a five-star bill. Most visitors, however, will find that three-star hotels are perfectly adequate for their needs, offering a comfortable room with bathroom en suite. The grading system is not always a totally reliable guide to room quality – even four- or three-star hotels have some rooms that are small, dark and cramped and, vice versa, a one- or two-star hotel may have one or two pricey rooms. As a rule, therefore, it is well worth having a look at the bedroom before committing yourself.

By law, foreigners are still required to register with the police on arrival in any Italian town, but in practice the hotel will do this automatically, taking your passport when you arrive to fill in the necessary form. There is also a tourist tax but this will be included in the price of your room, which should be clearly displayed in the room itself. Breakfast is very rarely included in the room price – in any case, hotel breakfasts, except in the most expensive hotels, are rarely worth eating; you would do better to follow the habit of locals and take coffee in a local bar.

One of several grand turn-of-the-century hotels in Florence

AGRITURISMO (FARM HOLIDAYS)

The changing pattern of rural economics means that more and more farmers are providing tourist accommodation to boost their incomes, sometimes in their homes and sometimes in converted barns and outbuildings. The whole idea of *Agriturismo* is that you should experience farm life (and you often eat with the host family) so you need to speak reasonably good Italian to make the most of it, although some farms offer self-catering accommodation. Details of Agriturismo holidays are to be found in the Annual Register of Tuscan Accommodation (see *Annuario* on page 174). There are three agencies in Florence: *Agriturist*, Piazza San Firenze 3 Florence (tel: 055 287 838); *Turismo Verde Toscana*, Via Verdi 5 (tel: 055 234 4751); and *Terranostra*, Via dei Magazzini 2 (tel: 055 214 430).

ALBERGHI PER LA GIOVENTU (YOUTH HOSTELS)

There are 12 youth hostels in Tuscany, but some of them are only open during the summer (from Easter to the end of September). There is no age limit for the use of these hostels (in fact senior citizens get discounts!) and you can join on the spot by buying a guest card from any hostel. With the exception of the Santa Monica hostel in Florence, all will provide meals. They are usually closed during the day from 10am to 6pm and facilities tend to be basic.

For further details, contact the head office for a map and list of hostel addresses: Associazione Alberghi per la Gioventu, Palazzo della Civilta del Lavoro, Quadrato della Concordia, 00144 Roma (tel: 06 593 1702).

Rustic style in San Gimignano

ALBERGO DIURNO (DAY HOTEL)

This highly civilised facility, which you would expect more countries to adopt, is, unfortunately, an endangered species even in the country of its origin. The day hotel is a boon of incalculable value to the traveller passing through a city. Open from 6am to midnight, the *albergo diurno* will provide all that you would expect to find in an ordinary hotel but without overnight accommodation. The *albergo diurno* at Montecatini Terme railway station, for instance, even has baths supplied with water from the spa. Usually day hotels are located in, or very close to, the main railway station.

ANNUARIO DELLE STRUTTURE RICETTIVE DELLA TOSCANA (ANNUAL REGISTER OF TUSCAN ACCOMMODATION)

This comprehensive annual publication is an invaluable reference work (with text in Italian, French, German, Spanish and English). It is far more than just a simple listing of hotels – it also covers holiday villages, farmhouse accommodation, trekking centres and camping sites. It is divided into the 13 official tourist districts of Tuscany, and each section includes a useful map of the area.

Running to over 700 pages, the Annuario is not the kind of handbook the average traveller will want to carry around, but it is very useful for advance planning and every hotel will have its own copy, so if you want to look something up just ask at the reception.

CHAINS

There are two Italian hotel chains that are worth knowing about. One of them is called CIGA (Compagnia Italiana Grandi Alberghi). Launched in Venice in 1906, CIGA specialises in taking over historic buildings and restoring them to the very highest standard. CIGA owns two five-star hotels in Florence, the Grand and the Excelsior (they actually face each other across the small Piazza Ognissanti). Both have been restored to their sumptuous 19th-century appearance and are worth a visit for their architecture alone. The other chain is the Family Hotels and Restaurants, Via Faenza 77, Firenze (tel: 055 217 975). This is an association of independent hotels which all have in common the fact that they are family-run. Many are in 17th- to 18th-century buildings and are graded three-star.

LOCANDA

The *locanda* is the cheapest form of accommodation apart from youth hostels. In a village or small town it could consist of a couple of rooms above a restaurant. In a large city it is more frequently a room in a family home. Using a *locanda* brings you into direct contact with the locals, so you need some knowledge of spoken Italian. Local tourist offices will give you details of *locanda* in their area.

MONASTERIES AND PILGRIM HOSTELS

The monastic tradition is still strong in Italy, and you do not have to be religiously inclined to take advantage of monastic hospitality – all you have to do is pay a very modest sum for lodgings. If there is no fixed charge you should make a donation equivalent to the rate for a one-star hotel (around 24,000 lire). Check with the local tourist boards what is available in the area.

In Siena the Casa del Pellegrino in the Santuario di Santa Caterina offers delightful accommodation with views across the city. Although run by nuns it has accommodation for both sexes; ring the bell by the gate in Via Camporegio (tel: 0577 44177). The only restriction is that you must be in by 11pm and you cannot get out before 8am without prior arrangement.

The Convento di Sant' Agostino, in Piazza di Sant' Agostino in San Gimignano, does not even have this restriction. You are given a key to the vast outside door of the cloister, and you can come and go as you please in the rambling guest wing. Both men and women are accommodated here (there are even double rooms) and you pay on arrival (tel: 0577 940 383).

Hotel and villa complex in Chianti created from converted farm buildings

VILLAGGI TURISTICI (TOURIST VILLAGES)

These are groups of custom-built bungalows and apartments, usually located near a popular resort. The bungalows vary in size but usually accommodate four people. Restaurant facilities are available on the site. The Annual Register of Tuscan Accommodation (see *Annuario* on page 174) contains full details.

VILLAS

The tremendous wave of building in the 16th and 17th centuries, when every family of substance expected to own a country retreat, has left a legacy of fine rural buiuldings all over Tuscany, many of which are now let as self-catering accommodation, complete with swimming pool and gardens (some even come complete with servants). The rental costs look high but can work out very reasonably if the party is large enough. Most major travel agents can arrange bookings and specialist agencies (as well as indiviudal owners) advertise in the classified sections of several leading British newspapers.

THOMAS COOK
Traveller's Tip

Travellers who purchase their travel tickets from a Thomas Cook network location are entitled to use the services of any other Thomas Cook network location, free of charge, to make hotel reservations.

On Business

*I*taly, in 1945, had endured the gimcrack Fascist regime of the 1930s, followed by the terrible hammering of World War II; it was now one of the poorest countries in Europe. Some four decades later, the Italian economy was growing faster than that of Britain and France. The Italians proudly call this *Il Sorpasso* (the 'overtaking') and emerged as one of the seven most powerful industrial nations in the world. Currently the country is experiencing the problems of corruption, in the business and political sphere, and of recession, but no one who knows Italy's track record can doubt but that it will emerge triumphant. *La dolce vita* plays no part in Italian businesses: they are formidable competitors.

An example of Italy's ability to adapt to changing conditions is its attitude to agriculture, the traditional industry. In 1950 it represented 25 per cent of the economy; in 1990 just 4 per cent. The other 21 per cent has been taken up by industries using new technologies. Italian industry is composed of a handful of giants operating on an international scale, then a band of some 3,500 middle-range firms. Beneath this is a multiplicity of small – frequently one-man operations – underpinning the whole.

ETIQUETTE

Despite the vigorous adoption of new technologies, doing business in Italy means observing traditional customs. Thus, while personal contact is extremely important, it is regarded as the height of bad manners to mix business and pleasure. Do not attempt to do business over a meal, particularly if you are a guest. Wine is central to Italian social life, but drunkeness is rare and regarded with contempt. It is customary to shake hands all round on meeting, and on departure. Titles should always be used. All university graduates, for instance, expect to be addressed as *Dottore* or *Dottoressa*, lawyers as *Avvocato*, architects as *Architetto*, engineers as *Ingegnere*. It is not necessary to use the surname with the title. The Tuscans are very fashion conscious and judge people by their appearance; you will gain greater credibility by dressing well.

WORKING HOURS

Lombardy has decided to break with the working hours of the past (which involved a 3-hour lunch break) and work the same hours as the rest of Europe, that is from 9am to 5.30pm. The rest of Italy has yet to follow suit, but more and more businesses are beginning to see the benefits. Where new working hours have yet to be established, office hours run from 8.30am to about 1pm and from 4.30pm to 7pm or even 8pm. Government offices are only open to the public in the morning. The custom of opening on Saturday morning is rapidly disappearing in favour of the *sabato inglese* ('the English Saturday'). Rather than take work home, however, an Italian would prefer to work in the office on Saturday or even a Sunday to clear a backlog. August is the official holiday month all over Italy and it is all but useless to try and make any appointments for this period.

INFORMATION

The Foreign Department (*Commercio Estero*) of the Chamber of Commerce (*Camera di Commercio*) in Florence will provide information on local industries: Piazza dei Giudici 3: (tel: 055 279 5275). Other Chambers are: Arezzo, Via Giotto 4 (tel: 0575 28891); Pisa, Piazza V Emanuele II 5 (tel: 050 512 111); Prato, Via Valentini 14 (tel: 0574 26061); Siena, Piazza Matteotti 30 (tel: 0577 45051).

Newspapers

Italy's two main daily newspapers, both carrying in-depth business news, are *La Repubblica* and *Corriera della Sera*. Two other papers are devoted enitrely to financial affairs – the daily newspaper *Il Sole–24 Ore* and the weekly *Italia Oggi*.

SERVICES

Executive Services, Via Ponte alle Mosse 61 (tel: 055 352 086); translators, secretaries and office space.
Centro Conit (tel: 055 583 675); secretarial and translation services.

EXHIBITIONS AND TRADE FAIRS

Several historic buildings in Florence have been converted to provide facilities for exhibitions and trade fairs. One of them is the Palazzo Strozzi, the venue for one of the biggest and most important antique trade fairs in Italy – the Mostra Mercato Internazionale dell'Antiquariato, held every autumn in odd-numbered years. In addition, there is the huge fortezza da Basso alongside the railway station, built in 1534. After use as a barracks and prison, it was converted to an exhibition centre in 1967. The interior of the fortress was transformed in 1978 when a new and modernistic exhibition hall was built of steel and aluminium. This is the venue for the prestigious Pitti Modo fashion shows held every year and the Mostra dell'Artigianato, a major exhibition of Tuscan art and craftsmanship.

Full information about the annual programme of trade fairs in Tuscany can be obtained from the tourist office (see page 189).

Practical Guide

CONTENTS

ARRIVING

Passports

To enter Italy, visitors from the USA, EC and Commonwealth countries need only a valid passport. Other nationals should apply for a visa in advance from an Italian embassy.

By air

Florence Peretola airport is 4km to the northwest of the city. Meridiana operates daily scheduled services to this airport from the UK, Spain, France, Germany and Belgium, and some tour operators offer charter flights in summer. For Peretola information tel: 055 373 498.

Pisa's Aeroporto Galileo Galilei is the main international airport for the region. This is a small, friendly airport well served by scheduled and charter flights from all over Europe. Opening times of facilities vary – foreign exchange is available from 8am to 6pm (not Sundays). Special toilets and phones are provided for disabled travellers. For flight information tel: 050 500707.

It is a short drive from Pisa airport to the two main motorways serving Tuscany, the A12 coastal autostrada and the A11 for Florence and Arezzo. Rail services connect the airport station hourly with Pisa (5 minutes) and Florence (56 minutes) and with Lucca, Montecatini, Pistoia and Prato (three times daily).

Any Thomas Cook Network location will offer airline ticket rerouting and revalidation free of charge to Mastercard holders and to travellers who have purchased their travel tickets from Thomas Cook.

By rail

The Thomas Cook European Timetable (tables 352 to 406) is invaluable for rail users travelling to, and within, Tuscany.

Overnight trains, with sleepers, leave daily from Paris Lyon on separate routes for Pisa and Florence (12 hours).

By road

The most comfortable way to take your car to Italy is by Motorail. Join at Calais, Bolougne, Dieppe or Paris and travel overnight to Livorno. The price may seem expensive but you will save greatly on petrol, overnight accommodation and frayed nerves. Britain is at least 48 hours from Tuscany by road.

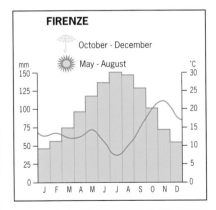

FIRENZE

October - December

May - August

mm		°C
150		30
125		25
100		20
75		15
50		10
25		5
0	J F M A M J J A S O N D	0

WEATHER CONVERSION CHART
25.4mm = 1 inch
°F = 1.8 × °C + 32

CAMPING

There are over 200 registered camping sites in Tuscany, with the highest concentration along the coast. The invaluable *Annuario delle Strutture e Ricettive della Toscana* (see page 174) provides full details. Overseas visitors can make advance bookings by writing for official forms to Centro Internazionale Prenotazione Federcampeggio, Casella Postale 23, 50041, Calenzano, Firenze (tel: 055 882 391).

CHILDREN

Children under four travel free on the railway and pay half the fare between the ages of four and 12.

CLIMATE

April to June and September to October are the best times to visit Tuscany. July and August, when the whole country is reeling under the heat, are the best months to avoid, particularly if you are planning to stay in the cities. The holiday season ends abruptly on 30 September in purely touristic resorts, such as the seaside. Rain can be expected at any time during autumn, but most often in September and November. October can be the ideal month of mild sunny days – and as hotel prices, too, are reduced after September an October holiday can well repay the gamble.

Conversion Table

FROM	TO	MULTIPLY BY
Inches	Centimetres	2.54
Feet	Metres	0.3048
Yards	Metres	0.9144
Miles	Kilometres	1.6090
Acres	Hectares	0.4047
Gallons	Litres	4.5460
Ounces	Grams	28.35
Pounds	Grams	453.6
Pounds	Kilograms	0.4536
Tons	Tonnes	1.0160

To convert back, for example from centimetres to inches, divide by the number in the third column.

Men's Suits

UK	36	38	40	42	44	46	48
Rest of Europe	46	48	50	52	54	56	58
US	36	38	40	42	44	46	48

Dress Sizes

UK	8	10	12	14	16	18
France	36	38	40	42	44	46
Italy	38	40	42	44	46	48
Rest of Europe	34	36	38	40	42	44
US	6	8	10	12	14	16

Men's Shirts

UK	14	14.5	15	15.5	16	16.5	17
Rest of Europe	36	37	38	39/40	41	42	43
US	14	14.5	15	15.5	16	16.5	17

Men's Shoes

UK	7	7.5	8.5	9.5	10.5	11
Rest of Europe	41	42	43	44	45	46
US	8	8.5	9.5	10.5	11.5	12

Women's Shoes

UK	4.5	5	5.5	6	6.5	7
Rest of Europe	38	38	39	39	40	41
US	6	6.5	7	7.5	8	8.5

CRIME

Florence and Pisa, with their large populations and heavy tourist concentrations, are the places where, if at all, the tourist will encounter crime. Even here you are extremely unlikely to be the object of violent crime. The worst problem you are likely to encounter is the activity of skilful and remarkably audacious pickpockets. If you are robbed you should make an official report to the police. They will not take much interest and it is unlikely that you will get your property back, but you must obtain an official statement in order to claim insurance. Multi-lingual statement forms are available at the main police station in Florence: Questura, Via Zara 2 (tel: 055 49 771) and in Pisa: Questura, Via M Lalli (tel: 050 583 511).

CUSTOMS REGULATIONS

Since January 1992 these have largely been abolished for citizens of EC countries. Others visitors are entitled to the duty free allowances shown below:
Goods obtained duty and tax free within the EEC:
300 cigarettes or 75 cigars or 400g of tobacco.
Alcohol: over 22% volume: 1 litre; under 22%: 2 litres; ordinary table wine: 2 litres.
Perfume: 50g.
Toilet water: 250cc.
Travellers under 17 years of age are not entitled to the drink and tobacco allowances.

DISABLED TRAVELLERS

Individual Italians are helpful but there is little done officially to help the disabled. Ramps, lifts and chairlifts are only found in the mainstream tourist sights (such as the Uffizi and the Duomo in Florence). It is virtually impossible for disabled people to use the railway without help because of the height of the carriage door above the platform. RADAR (The Royal Association for Disability and Rehabilitation) publishes a useful annual guide called *Holidays and Travel Abroad* detailing facilities. Write to RADAR, 25 Mortimer Street, London W1N 8AB (tel: 071 637 5400).

DRIVING

The major cities of Tuscany, such as Florence, Siena and Pisa, are no place for the timid driver. Parking is difficult in these cities and traffic is excluded from the centre. On the other hand, a car is essential if you want to get off the beaten track and explore rural Tuscany.

Accidents

In the event of an accident, exchange insurance information with the driver(s) of other vehicle(s) involved, inform the police and make a statement and inform your insurance company. Most hire car companies have a ready-made form with carbon copy to be filled in by both parties in the case of an accident.

Autostrade

Italian motorways are excellent but you pay for the priviledge of using them. When you join a motorway, you will pass through a barrier; stop and press the large red button on the left (driver's side) and you will be issued with a ticket. Hand this in at the booth when you exit the motorway and an illuminated display will tell you what to pay.

Breakdown

Switch the hazard warning lights on immediately and place the red warning triangle 50m behind the vehicle. Find a telephone and ring 116, the number for the Automobile Club d'Italia (ACI). Members of AIT or FIA affiliated motoring clubs with an assistance booklet will be assisted under the 'Snake' agreement. All other motorists must pay the regular cost. It is well worth using this number too if you have an accident; the ACI will help with police formalities and the exchange of insurance details. If necessary they will also help to find a garage for repairs.

There are double telephones on the *autostrade*: the one with a picture of a wrench is for reporting mechanical problems and the one with the red cross is for calling an ambulance. The road police (*polizia stradale*) patrol frequent.

Documents

If you hold an old green UK license you must obtain and carry an official translation (from AA offices). No translation is necessary if you hold a pink Euro license. If you are driving your own car in Italy you will need to carry the registration and MOT documents and an international green insurance card. If you are hiring a car in Italy, the rental company will supply these.

Parking

Scarcely any town or city in Tuscany allows cars into the inner city area and there is never enough space in the perimeter car parks to cope with demand in summer. This means that you should arrive at your destination as early in the day as possible to be sure of finding a space. In Florence, the major car parks are all near the main railway station. Where there are blue lines you must pay the attendant.

Petrol

Petrol prices in Italy are among the highest in Europe. Petrol stations are usually open from 7.30am to noon and 4pm to 7pm, Monday to Friday. Many (75 per cent) are closed on Saturday and Sunday, and all close on public holidays, except for autostrade service stations.

Some petrol stations display a sign saying Aperto 24 Ore; this means that they have an automatic pump which accepts 10,000 lire notes. Very few petrol stations accept credit cards. Two types of petrol are sold: Super (4-star) and Super senza piombo (unleaded). Diesel is sold as gasolio.

Rental

There are plenty of travel agents offering fly-drive packages to Pisa, where cars can be collected on arrival at the airport. The price should include unlimited mileage and insurance as well as a 24-hour emergency breakdown service. Indivdual hire companies in Tuscany include the following.

Florence: Avis, Borgo Ognissanti 128R (tel: 050 213 629); Europcar, Borgo Ognissanti 53R (tel: 055 293 444); Hertz, Via Maso Finiguerra 33 (tel: 055 239 8205.

Pisa Airport: Autotravel (tel: 050 46209); Avis (tel: 050 42028); Europcar (tel: 050 41017); Maggiore (tel: 050 42574).

Pisa: Avis, Lungarno Guadalongo 3 (tel: 050 42327); Hertz, Via Vespucci 106a (tel: 050 40878 or 44389).

Maggiore now have an office at Peretola airport (Florence).

Rules of the road

Traffic drives on the right and the speed limits are 50kmh in built-up areas, 90kmh on secondary roads, 110kmh on motorways and 130kmh on the *autostrada*. Seat belts must be worn in the front of the car and by children in the rear. Using the horn is prohibited in built-up areas except in emergencies; flash your lights instead as a warning. Outside towns use the horn to warn that you are about to overtake and to warn of your presence on a blind bend.

ELECTRICITY

The supply is 220 volts and most sockets take two-pin plugs. Adaptors are required for most non-Continental appliances and a transformer if the appliances normally operate at 100–120 volts (eg US and Canadian standard).

EMBASSIES AND CONSULATES

Most are in Rome; UK and USA maintain consulates in Florence.

UK, Lungarno Corsini 2 (tel: 284 133); USA, Lungarno Amerigo Vespucci 38 (tel: 055 239 8276).

EMERGENCY TELEPHONE NUMBERS

Fire, Police and Ambulance: tel: 113. Thomas Cook travellers' cheque refund (24-hour service – report loss or theft within 24 hours): 1678 72050 (local call rates).

ETIQUETTE

Visitors are expected to be decently dressed, especially when entering churches. Shorts and beachware are frowned upon and the quality of service and respect you receive goes up if you dress smartly.

HEALTH

All EC countries have reciprocal arrangements for reclaiming the costs of medical services. UK residents should obtain forms CM1 and E111 from any post office in the UK. This provides detailed information as to how to claim and what is covered. Claiming is often a laborious and long drawn-out process and you are only covered for medical care, not for emergency repatriation, holiday cancellation, and so on. You are therefore strongly advised to take out a travel insurance policy to cover all eventualities. You can purchase such insurance through the AA, branches of Thomas Cook and most travel agents.

Tuscany presents no health hazards that cannot be avoided by using common sense. Mosquitoes and other biting insects are the major nuisance and some form of repellent, as well as ointment to soothe bites, is a good idea. The summer sun is very fierce and you should adopt a cautious approach to sunbathing. Pharmacists are well-qualified to give advice on any minor ailments. If you need emergency help call *Pronto Soccorso* (First Aid) tel: 113.

LANGUAGE
Pronunciation

A as in father.
E as in egg.
I like e in easy.
O as in ostrich.
U like oo as in food.
C or cc before e or i is pronounced ch, as in church. Otherwise c, cc and ch are prounced k, as in cake.
G is soft as in ginger when followed by i or e, but hard as in go in all other cases.

The accent is nearly always on the penultimate syllable; there are few exceptions to this rule and you will sometimes see them indicated by an accent as in città. Most feminine words end in a (plural e): masculine words end in o (plural i). The definite article is *la* (feminine) and *il* (masculine).

General

Si yes
No no
Grande large/big
Piccolo small
Buono good
Cattivo bad
Bene well
Va' bene everything's fine
Quanto? how much?
Troppo too much
Molto very much
Basta enough
Aperto open
Chiuso closed
Biglietto ticket
Entrata entrance
Uscita exit
Sinistra left
Destra right
Dove? where?
Dov'e? where is?
Quando? when?
Ferrovie railway

Useful phrases
Parla inglese? Do you speak English?
Non capisco I do not understand
Chi parla inglese? Who speaks
English (here)?
Parla lentamente Speak slowly
Per favore Please
Grazie Thank you
Prego Please (don't mention it) the
invariable response to 'grazie'
Permesso! Excuse me! (eg when
moving through a crowd)
Mi scusi Excuse me (apology)
Mi dispiace I am sorry
Niente Nothing/it does not matter
Come si chiama? What is your
name/what is this called?

Numbers

Uno	one
Due	two
Tre	three
Quattro	four
Cinque	five
Sei	six
Sette	seven
Otto	eight
Nove	nine
Dieci	ten
Cento	hundred

Days of the week

Lunedì	Monday
Martedì	Tuesday
Mercoledì	Wednesday
Giovedì	Thursday
Venerdì	Friday
Sabato	Saturday
Domenica	Sunday

Food and drink

Aceto	vinegar
Acqua	water
Agnello	lamb
Ananas	pineapple
Anatra	duck
Arancia	orange
Asparagi	asparagus
Bicchiere	glass
Bottiglia	bottle
Burro	butter
Ceci	chick peas
Conto	the bill
Coniglio	rabbit
Fagioli	haricot beans (*all'olio* with olive oil; *all'uccelletto* with garlic and tomatoes)
Fagiolini	green beans (usually served cold with olive oil)
Fichi	figs
Formaggio	cheese
Fragole	strawberries
Macedonia	fruit salad
Manzo	beef
Mele	apple
Oliol	oil
Pane	bread
Peperoni	sweet peppers
Pera	pear
Pesca	peach
Piselli	green peas
Rognoni	kidneys
Sarde	sardines
Seppia	cuttle fish
Spinaci	spinach
Tonno	tuna
Trota	trout
Uva	grapes
Vino	wine (*rosso* red, *bianco* white, *rosa* rose)
Vitello	veal

LOST PROPERTY

Thomas Cook (Italia) Ltd, Ponte Vecchio, Lungarno Acciauoli 6r Florence, will provide emergency assistance for loss or theft of MasterCard credit cards or Thomas Cook travellers' cheques. Report other losses or theft to the police (see **Crime**, page 180).

UK and US citizens can contact their consulates in Florence for emergency assistance or advice (see **Embassies and Consulates**, page 183). Florence has a central lost property office: Ufficio Oggetti Smarriti, at Via Circondaria 19 (tel: 055 367 943).

MAPS

Local tourist offices (see page 190) will provide town maps free of charge.

MEDIA

Tuscany's main newspaper is *La Nazione*. This is published in Florence but there are regional inserts dealing with local news and events for each of Tuscany's nine provinces. Newspapers from other parts of Europe are widely available on the same day, or the day after publication.

Two English-language newspapers, *The International New York Herald Tribune* (daily) and *The European* (weekly) regularly carry sections dealing with Italian affairs and these give a useful summary of what is happening in the country as a whole. Most large hotels in Florence will have copies of the free listings publication (in English and Italian) called *Concierge Information* which carries up-to-date information on entertainment, tours, shopping and the like. Florence also has an Italian-language listings publication called *Firenze Spettacolo* .

MONEY MATTERS

The Italian lira (plural lire) is usually abbreviated to L or £. The lira is a relatively stable currency and exchange rates have not fluctuated much in recent years.

Notes come in denominations of 1,000, 2,000, 5,000, 10,000, 50,000 100,000 lire; coins in denominations of 50, 100, 200 and 500 lire. Telephone tokens (*gettoni*) are also accepted as coinage: their current value is 200 lire.

Banks are open weekdays from 8.30am to 1pm. Some city centre banks also open in the afternoon from 3pm to 4pm. None open at weekends. Most large hotels will change travellers' cheques without difficulty. All major railway stations have an exchange kiosk (signposted *cambio*). The Thomas Cook Florence office at Ponte Vecchio (for address see **Lost Property**) changes Thomas Cook travellers' cheques free of commission, as well as offering all other bureau de change facilities.

The major credit cards are widely accepted and automatic cash dispensers are increasingly common. Travellers' cheques can be used to settle bills and are the safest way to carry money.

The major credit cards (Visa,

MasterCard/Access, American Express and Diners' Club) are accepted in many hotels and restaurants and up-market shops (look for a sign saying *Carta Si – Card Yes* – in the window). Despite the high price of petrol, however, very few garages accept cards. You will also have to pay cash for your groceries; small shops only accept cash and the out-of-town hypermarkets issue their own charge cards and only accept these.

Eurocheques are very widely accepted in Italy and are as good as money: each cheque can be cashed at a bank for up to 300,000 lire. Neither will any problem be encountered with cashing travellers' cheques, though for all bank transactions it is necessary to present your passport.

When looking for the best possible rates of exchange, it is usually advantageous to use bank or credit cards, because the exchange calculation is done at the inter-bank rate, which is more favourable than the tourist rate. Most banks in Italy also charge a small commission for changing cash or Eurocheques, though visitors should not be charged for cashing a travellers' cheque.

NATIONAL HOLIDAYS

All government offices and banks, most other offices and all the larger shops are closed on the following days:
1 January
6 January (Epiphany)
Easter Monday
25 April (Liberation Day)
1 May (Labour Day)
15 August (Feast of the Assumption)
1 November (All Saints)
8 December (Feast of the Immaculate Conception)
25 and 26 December

In addition, virtually every locality will celebrate its own patron saint's feast day. When this happens, everything closes for at least that day, and often the day before and the day after as well.

OPENING HOURS

In general, all government-run organisations (including many museums and tourist offices), as well as many banks close for the day at 1pm. Some banks in the larger towns may open again for an hour in the afternoon, usually between 3pm and 4pm. Shops also close at 1pm but are open again from 3.30pm or 4pm until 7pm.

ORGANISED TOURS

The tourist offices in Florence and Pisa will put you in touch with individual guides who will charge up to L200,000 per day. They have to pass rigorous tests and are very good. The following agencies specialise in tours (usually by coach) to the major sights of Tuscany and beyond.

Florence

Chiariva, Borgo Santi Apostoli 9 (tel: 055 211 968); CIT Viaggi, Via Cavour 56r (tel: 055 294 306); Eyre e Humbert, Via del Parione 56r: (tel: 055 238 2251); Firenze Tours, Via Montebello 1r (tel: 055 218 560); Primavera Viaggi, Via Ricasoli 9 (tel: 055 282 042).

Pisa

Agenzia Viaggi il Delfino, Lungarno Gambacorti 28 (tel: 050 48801); Escapade, Via Notari 15 (tel: 050 500 368); Meloria Viaggi, Via A Frati 19 (tel: 050 502 211); Toscana Vacanze, Via Ridolfi 34 (tel: 055 575 777); Turitalia, Via Turati 24 (tel: 050 24562).

PHARMACIES

These are indicated by a green cross sign and concentrate on selling pharmaceutical products. Cosmetics and the like will be found in a *profumeria*. The location of the nearest late-night pharmacy is indicated by a notice posted in the window of all pharmacies. Florence has an organisation called *Associazione Volontari Ospedalieri* (AVO) which provides free interpreters in case of medical emergencies (tel: 055 403 126).

PLACES OF WORSHIP.

American Episcopal Church of St James, Via B Rucellai 9, Florence(tel: 055 294 417). All services are in English.
Church of England, Via Maggio, 16, Florence (tel: 055 294 764).
Christian Adventist, Via Guelfa 12, Florence (tel: 055 495882).
Evangelical Baptist, Borgo Ognissanti, 4, Florence (tel: 055 210 537).
Evangelical Lutheran, Lungarno Torrigiano, 11, Florence (tel: 055 234 2775).
Evangelical Church of the Brethren, Via della Vigna Vecchia, 15/17, Florence (tel: 055 217 236).
First Church of Christian Scientists, Via F Baracca, Florence (tel: 055 432 383).
Jewish, Via L C Farini 4, Florence (tel: 055 245252).

Methodist, Via de' Benci 9, Florence (tel: 055 292673).
Salvation Army, Via Aretina, 91, Florence (tel: 055 660 445).

POLICE

Somewhat confusingly, Italy has several different types of police force. The *Carabinieri* are an armed, paramilitary force operating throughout the country and directly concerned with serious crime. The *Guardia di Finanza* also have countrywide powers and they are mainly concerned with fraud, tax evasion and corruption. The *Polizia dello Stato* are responsible for policing major cities and their police station (called a *questura*) is where you go to report theft and petty crime. The *Polizia Stradale* patrol the *autostrade* and main roads. The body with whom the visitor is most likely to come into contact is the *Polizia Muncipale* or the *Vigili Urbani* who are mainly concerned with preventing parking offences and the like.

POSTAL SERVICES

The Italian postal system is notoriously strike ridden and inefficient. You can be reasonably certain of being home well before any postcards you send. Avoid post offices if you possibly can – long queues and poor service are endemic. Instead go to a tobacconist or stationer for stamps (*francobolli*). If you have to visit a post office, they are at Via Pelliceria in Florence (*open: 8.30am– 7pm*) and Piazza Vittorio Emanuele in Pisa (*open: 8.15am– 7.30pm*).

PUBLIC TRANSPORT

This is one of the few public services in Italy that is reliable; it is also relatively cheap and wideranging – there are few places in Tuscany that cannot be reached by bus or train.

Long-distance coaches and buses

LAZZI, Piazza Stazione 4, Florence (tel: 055 215 154).
LAZZI, Piazza Vittorio Emanuele II, Pisa: (tel: 050 46288).
SITA, Via Caterina da Siena 15, Florence (tel: 055 483 651). For weekday information on local coaches ring 483651, and 211487 for Saturday and Sunday.
TRA-IN, Piazza San Domenico, Siena (tel: 0577 221 221).

Railway

Tickets must be bought before you board. If you are caught without a ticket on board there is an automatic fine of at least 20 per cent of the ticket price. There are several different types of train.

Inter City, Super *Rapido* and *Rapido* trains are the fastest, stopping only at major cities; when buying your ticket you must specify that you are taking one of these trains because there is a supplement of 30 per cent which must also be paid before boarding the train. They are indicated on train noticeboards by the letters IC or R. *Espresso* and *Diretto* trains stop at most large stations while the *Locale* train stops at every station. There are three main types of rail pass which provide savings: Travel at

Will (*Biglietto Turistico Libera Circolazione*) covers the entire rail network for periods ranging from eight to 30 days; *Flexicard* is cheaper and covers the same ground but with more limited validity; the *Kilometric* entitles you to 20 journeys or a maximum of 3,000km of travel. All are available through most travel agents.

SENIOR CITIZENS

European Community citizens who have reached retirement age are entitled to free entry to state museums and galleries on production of a passport as evidence of their age.

STUDENT AND YOUTH TRAVEL

Italy makes few concessions to students. Discounted travel is available on Italian railways; details are available from most travel agents.

TELEPHONES

Coin and card-operated telephones are now almost universal and reasonably efficient (the old type of phone, operated by tokens, has almost disappeared). Booths are liberally distributed on city streets, and phones are also available in many bars. Phone cards can be bought in tobacconists and newsagents, and from machines in railway stations and

post offices. A very useful service for foreign visitors can be obtained by dialing 172 followed by the national code. This will connect you with an operator in your own country and you can then reverse the charges to your home or office telephone.

International codes:
Ireland 353
New Zealand 64
UK 44
US 1
Tuscany area codes: Arezzo 0575; Florence 055; Lucca 0583; Pisa 050; Pistoia 0573; Prato 0574; Siena 0577.

TIME
GMT is one hour behind Italian time all year except for a brief period in October when both times are equal.

TIPS
Most restaurants automatically add a service charge to your bill, but you can leave a little extra for exceptional service.

TOILETS
Most museums now have public toilets, as do railway stations and department stores. Toilets in cafés are there for customer use so do not barge in and demand to use them for free – if you do you will be told they are broken. Toilet in Italian is *bagno* and the gents' will be marked *signori* or *uomini*, the ladies' *signore or donne*.

TOURIST INFORMATION
Arezzo: Piazza della Repubblica, 28 (tel: 0575 20839). Open: Sunday to Friday, 9am–1pm and 3pm–6pm; Saturday, 9am–1pm. Also Piazza Risorgimento 116 (tel: 0575 23952).
Bagni di Lucca: Via Umberto 1, 139 (tel: 0583 87946).

Barga: Pro Loco Ufficio Informazione, Piazza Angelico, 2 (tel: 0583 723 499).
Carrara: Piazza Giugno, 2 (tel: 0584 843 370).
Chiusi: Via Porsenna, 61 (tel: 0578 227 667).
Fiesole: Piazza Mino, 37 (tel: 055 598 720).
Florence: Via Manzoni, 16 (tel: 055 23320). Main railway station. A little round marble kiosk on causeway behind the taxi rank.
Lucca: Piazza Guidiccioni, 2 (tel: 0583 491 205). More popular however are other offices: Via Veneto, 40 (tel: 0583 419 689/493 639) (SIP). Piazzale G. Verdi (tel: 0583 53592).
Montecatini: Viale G. Verdi, 66 (tel: 0572 772 244).
Montepulciano: Piazza Don Minzoni, 8 (tel: 0578 75742).
Pisa: Lungarno Mediceo, 42 (tel: 050 542 322). However, more popular: Piazza del Duomo (tel: 050 560 464). Piazza della Stazione (tel: 050 42291).
Prato: Via Cairoli, 48 (tel: 0574 24112).
Siena: Via di Citta, 43 (tel: 0577 42209). Piazza del Campo, (tel: 0577 280 551).
Viareggio: Viale G. Carducci (tel: 0584 48881).

ACKNOWLEDGEMENTS
The Automobile Association wishes to thank the following organisations, libraries and photographers for their assistance in the preparation of this book.

J ALLAN CASH PHOTOLIBRARY 55, 80
RUSSELL CHAMBERLAIN 22a, 22b, 22c
THE GRANDE HOTEL 172
ANTONIO LELLI 175
THE NATIONAL GALLERY 98
SPECTRUM COLOUR LIBRARY Cover, 28b, 67b, 116, 150a, 150b, 156, 163b
ZETA PICTURE LIBRARY (UK) LTD 6, 25, 50, 64, 65, 145, 148, 149, 151

The remaining photographs are held in the AA Photo Library with contributions from:

JERRY EDMANSON 14, 28a, 29a, 29b, 30, 33, 37, 38a, 38b, 41a, 41b, 43c, 46, 48, 49, 51, 54, 57, 58, 62, 63, 67a, 78, 83b, 88a, 89b, 95b, 99, 118, 121, 128b, 137, 138, 141, 146, 160, 163a, 167, 181
KEN PATERSON Inset, Spine, 1, 4, 5, 7, 11, 15, 16, 17, 18, 19, 22d, 23, 24, 29c, 31, 32, 34, 39, 42, 43a, 43b, 44a, 44b, 47a, 56a, 56b, 59, 61a, 61b, 66a, 66b, 69, 75, 77, 79, 81, 83a, 88b, 89a, 90, 91a, 91b, 93, 94, 101, 102, 104, 105, 106a, 106b, 107, 109, 111, 115, 117, 119, 123, 127, 128a, 130, 131, 132, 133, 134, 135, 136, 139, 140a, 140b, 142a, 143b, 144, 152, 153a, 153b, 154, 155, 157, 159, 162b, 169, 170, 171a, 171b, 182, 185, 187, 189
CLIVE SAWYER 13
BARRIE SMITH 35, 40, 41c, 45, 47b, 53, 147, 161b, 173, 179a, 188
ANTONY SOUTER 2, 95a, 112, 129, 142b, 143a, 161a, 162a, 164, 165a, 165b

The Automobile Association would also like to thank the Automobile Club d'Italia for their assistance in checking details in the Practical Guide.

Series adviser: Melissa Shales

Copy editor: Christopher Catling